AFRICA IN NARRATIVES

-

Smith and Ce [ed.]

AFRICAN

Library of Critical Writing

AFRICA IN NARRATIVES
Smith and Ce (Edited)

©African Library of Critical Writing
Print Edition
ISBN: 978-9-7837-0858-7

For information address:
Progeny (Press) International
Email: progeny.int@gmail.com
For: African Books Network
9 Handel Str.
AI EBS Nigeria WA
Email: handelbook@gmail.com

Marketing and Distribution in the US, UK,
Europe, N. America (Canada),
and Commonwealth countries by

 African Books Collective Ltd.
PO Box 721
Oxford OX1 9EN
United Kingdom
Email: orders@africanbookscollective.com

Contents

Preface

OUR *Africa in Narratives* critical volume further illuminates or proves, against the backdrop of attitudes toward nations deemed 'ethnic' or minorities,' that literature in Africa can lived up to the challenge of esthetic imagination to form an active, refreshing part of world cultural discourse. Some would have us believe that it is difficult to speak of traditions or distinctive national features in literatures 'so young and mutable.' But that was several years ago.

In any case similar viewpoints served the purpose of challenging local intelligentsia further along the frontiers of theoretical delineation of their literatures. Bernth Lindfors had pointed to an emerging national literature in Nigerian and South African writing. He had noted, for instance, that 'Nigeria with a population today of one hundred million has been Africa's most prolific producer of English language literature for the past forty years,' with 'definite trends and tendencies' becoming 'slowly discernible.' While we may not agree that the amount of writing generated in Nigeria by her civil war 'turned Nigerian literature in a direction decidedly different from that of other West African literatures' -as so-called national still subsisting within with the African experience are diachronic of literatures from, say, Kenya or Swaziland, or even the Diaspora- now we can commonly agree that African literature must continue to reflect the distinctive imaginative landscape of that continent defined by its collective colonial and national experience which, in trend and development, offers comparative significance to other literary movements of most of the western world.

It is the hope –and the goal– of this project, in spite of scholastic opinions and other contrary inclinations, that until African countries have evolved imaginatively beyond their present ephemeral stages of social and political turmoil not to talk of intellectual imitations of western thought, national literatures should be subject to the imperative of a continental –and hopefully intercontinental– cooperation. This conscious understanding, or the continuous reassessment of heritage, is borne from the vision which some of Africa's great founding fathers and thought leaders had so selflessly, and also courageously, espoused.

-CS and CC

Writers' Forum

Chapter One

Literature and Leadership Issues

C. Ce

I

MODERN Nigerian writing, like the post colonial state, has run full cycle for forty years and cycles ever after around the wheel of poverty and underdevelopment for which the country has become notorious. Many of her writers have often sounded like Rosse in Shakespeare's *Macbeth* lamenting the Scottish homeland during the tyranny of the usurper king: '...poor country/ Almost afraid to know itself. It cannot/ be called our mother, but our grave' (185). One member of the new generation of Nigerian poets sadly muses: 'Now that every state is enslaved/ and the rock stairs that we built/ crumble on our heads... what use are the memorial drums?' (Enekwe 10).

A small, neglected pamphlet dots the reference section of the Nigerian national library. *The Trouble with Nigeria* by Chinua Achebe begins in a language and tone that would annoy its countrymen, particularly the political cheerleaders:

> There is nothing basically wrong with the Nigerian land or climate or water or air or anything else. The Nigerian problem is the unwillingness or inability of its leaders to rise to the responsibility, to the challenge of personal example which are the hallmarks of true leadership. (1)

African literature parallels politics closely even as critics who argue from a cultural position of art for arts' sake may tend to overlook this literary sensitivity to issues of politics, nationhood and citizenship. Yet while the Nigerian literati have since decades of political self-determination been preoccupied with social and political paradigms, as if walking on the front line, the question is how far has the literature gone towards the education of society? After forty years of independence, in any case, the readership may not have improved. Many intellectuals, as noted years ago, read very little and any writer, at the risk of bigotry, may add that this is why the development of the nation is all talk and little progress. 'Time is a serious handicap,'

> But there are other limiting factors besides time. The habit of reading itself is clearly the most important, for if it were strongly developed in our intellectuals some of them at least would find the time. But the habit is simply not there. (*Creation* 29)

With the obvious lacunae in imaginative thinking is it surprising the vacuity of national leadership and the country's descent in redundancy syndrome? Coming to power in 1999 with boasts of a new deal for his countrymen, Nigerian president, Olusegun Obasanjo, typical of the military that tutored him, declared a campaign against corruption. Two years in the same course his country was to rank in the hall of infamy as one of the most corrupt in the world. It was not long after that the president reconciled his brief epiphany of public accountability with the corruptive demands of his own political survival in office. Few Nigerians would forget his glib reaction to the international exposition that the highest corruption emanated from the central government of the nation where the retired general had full control. It smacked of a remark by a central character in *Children of Koloko* inter alia:

Dogkiller was once quoted, off the record of course, as saying that all this grammar of development didn't belong to high matters of state since it didn't quite put the food on his table. (41)

Nothing, however, would more please the beneficiaries of Nigeria's brand of democracy than the aphorism: 'The worst democracy is better than the best military rule'. The mediocrity of this thought and its overall acceptance among them seem the prevailing order of a society with hardly any sign of transition – which leaves little to wonder why they run the worst democracy in the world. The literature of Africa leaves memories of this era of history that the populace should be glad to put behind them. An excerpt from Achebe's *No Longer at Ease* gives an insight to public corruption in Nigeria of the seventies:

Some forty miles or so beyond lbadan the driver suddenly said: 'Dees b--f police!' Obi noticed two policemen by the side of the road about three hundred yards away, signalling the lorry to a stop. 'Your particulars?' said one of them to the driver. ... The driver asked his passengers to get up. He unlocked the box and brought out a sheaf of papers. The policeman looked at them critically. 'Where your roadworthiness?' The driver showed him his certificate of roadworthiness. Meanwhile the driver's mate was approaching the other policeman. But just as he was about to hand something over to him Obi looked in their direction. The policeman was not prepared to take a risk; for all he knew Obi might be a C.I.D. man. So he drove the driver's mate away with great moral indignation. 'What you want here? Go way!'
Meanwhile the other policeman had found fault with the driver's papers and was taking down his particulars, the driver pleading and begging in vain. Finally he drove away, or so it appeared. About a quarter of a mile father up the road he stopped. 'Why you look the man for face when we want give um him two shillings?' he asked Obi.

'Because he has no right to take two shillings from you,' Obi answered.

'Na him make I no de want carry you book people,' he complained. 'Too too know na him de worry una. Why you put your nose for matter way no concern you? Now that policeman go charge me like ten shillings.' (40)

Here is how Ayi Kwei Armah reflects the same pandemic ravaging independent Ghana in a later novel, *The Beautyful ones are not yet born*:

A small bus, looking very new and neat in its green paint, came up to the barrier. One of the policemen casually waved it to a stop and then just as casually he walked away to join the others...The driver of the small green bus stepped down and walked carefully over toward the policemen. ... 'Constable,' he said, as he got to the policemen, 'my passengers. They are in a hurry.'

One of the policemen looked up and said, 'is that so?' ...

The driver understood. Without waiting to be asked for it he took out his license folder from his shirt pocket, brought out a cedi note from the same place, and stuck it in the folder. Then, with his back turned to the people waiting in the bus, the driver gave his folder, together with the bribe in it, to the policeman.

The policeman looked with long and pensive dignity at the license folder and at what was inside it. With his left hand he extracted the money, rolling it up dexterously into an easy little ball hidden in his palm, while with his right he made awkward calculating motions, as if he were involved in checking the honesty of the document he held. (182)

Literary accounts of everyday situations in societies of that time depict an attitude of citizen complicity in an obvious state of anomie. Interestingly, while Achebe's society and leaders seemed to give up on corruption Armah's did not. Ghana's Aegean stable was fairly cleansed in the Rawlings revolution and modern Ghana transited from the venal society as

11

presented in Armah's novel to one of the few stable and descent places in Africa. The Nigerian republic, on the contrary, has kept a steady, geometric progression in public corruption that threatens to drown her nationalities in the pool of its affliction. At present, it includes an executive that claims to fight but performs the Hecate dance around the monster with senators and assemblymen in line. It is this celebration of mediocrity, and a sadly mistaken pretension to greatness, that scholars identify as the bane of Nigerian leadership. Achebe notes:

> In June 1979 former Chancellor Helmut Schmidt of West Germany made this comment about his country: Germany is not a world power; it does not wish to become a world power.
> In August of the same year General Olusegun Obasanjo said of Nigeria during his "Thank You Tour" of Ogun State: Nigeria will become one of the ten leading nations in the world by the end of the century. (10)

The laughable declaration was made during military rule by those whose tendency for deception in the seventies altered very little after the nineties. Nigeria now at forty, with the distended bellies of democracy like Obasanjo and his PDP cabal steering the ship, still dons the garb of gargantuan folly. The foppery of mundane minds emerging presidents and lawmakers in the country has since become a recurring theme in the drama of its own undoing. During the eighties and nineties, there was spirited campaign for army generals to continue the leadership of the country under a civilian arrangement. Government-owned radio and television stations would point to an American general who became president as a good example. But they never acknowledged that in 1799, Thomas Jefferson, before he became president of the United States, had said:

I am relying for internal defense, on our militia solely, till actual invasion, and for such naval force only as may protect our coasts and harbors from such depredations...; and not for a standing army in time of peace, which may overawe the public sentiment; nor for a navy, which by its own expenses and eternal wars...will grind us with public burdens and sink us under them.

David Trask, on the defense of democracy in the United States, observes that the minuscule size of both services (Army and Navy) was a further guarantee of their almost invisible role in national political life and of the principle of civilian control (13). Trask notes:

The military profession also retained its strong commitment to civilian leadership. In 1948 General Dwight Eisenhower, while discouraging efforts of supporters to nominate him for presidency summarized the dominant views of the professional military. He insisted that 'the necessary and wise subordination of the military to civil power will be best sustained and ... people will have greater confidence that it is so sustained, when lifelong professional soldiers, in the absence of some obvious and overriding reasons, abstain from seeking high political office. (14)

And so with the conspiracy of May 1999 that grafted General Obasanjo to civilian leadership, Nigerians have paid the price of untold suffering and hardship which the military turncoat visited upon his people, with public outbursts so foolish, so uncharitable, and comparable only to the legendary notoriety of Idi Amin of Uganda. Which is probably why the president could run the most corrupt nation in the millennium and proclaim 'I dey kampe,' (Nigerian pidgin English meaning he's in control) to an early impeachment bid that could not see him out of office. And why the façade of his anti-corruption commission - rightly called his witch hunt machinery - meant

13

to gain him some regard among the comity of nations never convinced the civilised world.

Ethnicity and Education in Nigeria

Nigeria's multiethnic composition has been stated as the single most constraining factor in the evolution of that nation state. Its decline to civil tyranny under Obasanjo only confirms the desperate attempts since the first coup d'etat to keep a collapsing federation together. Undoubtedly the country has the largest concentration of ethnicities in Africa numbering well over three hundred and fifty two. The domination by the majorities on the point of still debated numerical strength has engendered much angst in that while the bulk of revenue generated through oil exports come predominantly from so-called delta 'minorities,' infrastructural development from oil income is squandered on Lagos and Abuja 'majorities.'

Currently the Niger delta region is being run like pre-revolution France where, as Peacock tells, peasants gave up their land in despair and took to brigandage and smuggling (6). With the youths of the delta turning to terrorism and other crimes lately, armed rebellion against the state, with more organised terrorist strategies, portends grim news for the future. The aggressive peasant groups of eighteenth century France were wont to be given shelter and protection by sympathetic villagers. That tax collectors were then murdered and soldiers constantly used to suppress food riots (7) echo present conditions in the delta where most have had their rights to decent life violated with the callousness and brutality of parasites and absentee landlords of medieval Europe. A young environmental poet writes what none will deign to read at the country's government houses:

First it was the Ogoni/ Today it is Ijaw/ Who will be slain this next
day/ We see open mouths/But hear no screams/ Tears don't flow/
When you are scarred/ We stand in pools/Up to our knees/ We
thought it was oil/But it was blood. (Blood 14)

Official history may proclaim that Nigeria survived a
fratricidal war of national unity but this was merely a war of
attrition by mutually antagonistic leaders and self-serving
decision makers at home and abroad. The conditions that led
to that war have since replicated in far worse dimensions.
Massacre of other ethnicities continues in the northern states
such as Kano, Kaduna, and Jos. Almost every northern state
has enjoyed the barbarism of slaughtering the southern
nationalities for reasons of religious differences and political
disagreements rooted in primordial ethnic chauvinism. Where
political murders and inter-tribal rivalry have not blown into
another war, they seethe in the cauldron of competing forces
striving for petty advantages to the detriment of the whole.
Inordinate ambitions and switching loyalties remain the
hallmark of its national and political life - leaving out the
international football where citizens seem to respond to a
common purpose. But there, too, the sports ministry, like
electric, power, steel and other national establishments, insures
its endemic failure with nepotism and corruption.

Ever since the educational sector blazed in ruins by
Northern-backed incendiary using the quota system, an avid
ethnocentric admissions policy as a rule became entrenched in
Nigerian tertiary institutions. Universities funded with 'federal'
resources began to clamour for mere sectional advancements
in a country that claimed to have fought to preserve her unity.
It was not long before other nationalities in their exuberance
copied the Northern policy. Thus the 1990s witnessed the final
crumbling of all that constituted its educational heritage as

foreign nations began to decertify the plethora of degrees awarded by Nigerian universities after 1989.

The sanction led by the United States may have been timely and appropriate in that the nineties was the apogee of bastardies in public educational systems. While the national institutions were overrun by ethnic lords of their various localities, the state-owned universities, sprung with the haphazardness of state creations, were determined mainly to produce as many graduates as can compete in federal labour positions. Standards and procedures for admissions were jettisoned for entrees that could never have passed senior high. In some educationally-disadvantaged states (one of Nigeria's jargons for elevating mediocrity above merit and quality) these half-baked certificate holders became teachers in their turn. Having neither the diligence of 'little frogies' who went to school nor 'polished' to any degree whatever, the local champions simply filled the vacant slots of their state towers as of right.

Nowadays it is common to find positions like departmental heads and faculty deans occupied by 'acting' misfits, or sitting professors with hardly any research contributions to society. Some universities in their rush to award higher degrees begin their postgraduate programs with barely a backward glance at prior undergraduate competency. Standards are jettisoned for third rate 'indigene' candidates in the academic race. Our tertiary institutions now produce graduates who reel out semi-literate clichés redolent with pidgin and American hip hop. Yet while United States may succeed by a trained and motivated force in combating their own mediocrity and gangsterdom in schools, ours will never know what to do with her own equivalents where high-ranking society's leaders are either members or founders and patrons of campus cults. The impact of degenerating education structures has taken its toll on citizens with the alarming rate of unemployed graduates, the collapse of the economy, and the erosion of tradition and values. These are the days when legislators, those active collaborators in national ruination who could afford to cart local currencies in large fibre-woven bags, now send their children and wards to study in neighbouring countries for qualitative education.

The Politics of Nationhood

It should be needful to state that the fourth attempt at democracy in Nigeria hijacked by the Peoples Democratic Party is a charade of society's dregs. These are either unenlightened military despots with claims to some level of education only available from their military schools, or a criminal gang of political hirelings, touts, jobbers, fraudsters and some academics who managed to commandeer the business of government to parade themselves as Nigeria's leaders at federal and state levels of government. From these have emerged Nigeria's past and present presidents, state governors, local council chairs, and, from 2004, an inane array of ministers, special advisers, commissioners and party leaders.

The queue for leadership succession equally comes from among these ranks as few enlightened statesmen and women decide not to tarnish their image in the craze for plunder of public resources preferring, instead, a more respectable opposition. Those in this category include writers and activists like Wole Soyinka, winner of Nobel Prize for Literature in 1988, Gani Fahewinmi, distinguished lawyer and social crusader, and Beko Ransome Kuti whose family had engaged in frontline struggles against the repression of the colonial ruling class, to name but a few. Unfortunately these members

17

that kept aloof from the charade that is Nigerian politics are few indeed. The literary maestro, Achebe, and distinguished diplomat, Emeka Anyaoku, have persistently resisted calls to join politics out of fear of being compromised by the vociferous majority of brigands that fill that class in Nigeria.

Many writers had warned that this methodised plundering could lead Africa to further abyss of darkness and despair. In the 1980s a Soyinka play entitled *The Beatification of Area Boy* captured the festering shame that Nigeria had metamorphosed under General Ibrahim Babangida (1985-1993) and General Sani Abacha (1994-1998) - two dictatorships that exceeded General Gowon's (1967-1975) in corruption and bestiality. Beatification soon became a mirror of modern Nigeria whose internal contradictions could, however, produce enlightened street kings such as Sanda only in the creative imagination. There is something in the mentality of 'Military Officer' in Beatification that resonates successively with Abacha's murdering of Ogoni dissenters and Obasanjo's executive pogrom at Odi and Benue. Here is an excerpt from *The Beatification of Area Boy*:

> SANDA. So Maroko is really gone? Gone for good?
> MILITARY OFFICER. Didn't you see the bonfire? We didn't merely bulldoze it, we dynamited every stubborn wall, then set fire to the rubble. That place was disease ridden! No point developing it for decent citizens only to have them die of some lingering viruses from way back. Those squatters might be immune to anything but we have to think of the future residents. We took them by surprise. They woke up as usual but found themselves staring into the muzzles of guns. Few of them had any time to pick up their belongings. (80)

Earlier in 1988, Achebe's *Anthills of the Savannah* had made a prophetic testimonial about the revisionism of the

Nigerian military that came to light in the nineties of Nigeria's political history. The strong point in these works by Soyinka and Achebe, easily ignored by many a reader of Nigerian writing, is that these leaders of state have been mere pretenders to charisma cheered by the usual motley band of sycophants. The second point is that the predilection for anomalies in various strains of government is sustained from the crude, destructive Unitarian structure that survives one regime after another in corruption and abuse of power. But since, as noted, Nigeria's ruling elite do not care for literature, or any creative work for that matter, there is hardly a hope that its liberating thought can ever coalesce in the form of a liberating philosophy. Insights garnered from the literature of their brightest minds to restructure the polity have been ignored. This witlessness is due to the inherent structure of the postcolonial state designed to suit the interests of unenlightened political godfathers and their serving mass of minions.

The prodigality of the PDP-led political regimen will persist as long as Nigeria's ethnic plurality ensures the rejection of holistic perspectives on issues that could turn the state around. National questions are often polarized along ethnicity, and then, around religious dichotomies. The British colonial government, not too aware of ancient African religions and traditions, sought to vilify them through their missionaries. While traditional life could absorb or blend peacefully with even the most fundamental thoughts, the divisive and violent northern Muslim and southern Christian affiliations that came with Imperialism have tended to bifurcate the country's tenuous federation. Nigerian leaders, perennially sprung from this haunted religious divide, and lacking in any nobility of spirit and altruism of vision, fail to counterbalance the centrifugal forces. Each leader rather appeals to a religiously brainwashed populace seemingly incapable of independent reasoning. Every leader retains a blanket attitude to religion and lip service to the secularity of state which have robbed the country of transformative possibilities.

With the religious attitude of Nigerians to problem solving technology can turn to a superstition. Despite its population advantage, the country remains backward in the use of online facilities. At the dawn of the 21st century the 'millennium bomb' became an atomic project that was programmed for divine destruction of the world. The abject disdain for contemporary challenges becomes the incentive for despotic regimes that have impoverished the country from the military rule of the eighties to the current chicanery of democracy. Nowadays many a Christian faithful can look forward to biblical Armageddon in its whole sense of Zionist racialism. Citing tendentious scriptures and rabbinical forgeries, black scholars of Christian or Muslim extractions promote beliefs in a Jewish or Palestinian ancestor - if only to spite more ancient records of human civilisation. This mental servitude is rooted in foreign religions that are here embraced with the fervency and unquestioning loyalty of uninformed populations.

Nigeria therefore became one of the most religious countries of the world not for spirituality or love of truth but mainly for competing Christian-Muslim interests and the primordial supremacy battles that rage between them in corridors of government. Paradoxically, news exposes this 'most religious' country, where the people consult their deities regularly, as a most dangerous, filthy and decadent enclave - a place where all manners of rituals thrive with executive complicity and, in the eyes of her neighbours, where ritual murders and cult patronage come from the rank of political leaders and government executives. One can agree no less with the supposition that such a country cannot be great, cannot attain greatness, nor ever have greatness thrust upon it, in spite of any religious faith or executive bravado; as Achebe states:

> Listen to Nigerian leaders and you will frequently hear the phrase this great country of ours.
> Nigeria is not a great country. It is one of the most disorderly nations in the world. It is one of the most corrupt, insensitive, inefficient places under the sun. It is one of the most expensive countries and one of those that give least value for money. It is dirty, callous, noisy, ostentatious, dishonest and vulgar. In short, it is among the most unpleasant places on earth! (Trouble 19)

State Brutality and the Police

Nigeria is clearly a police state in today's democracy where leaders or winners are selected from political drawing tables and executive lists. Under military command it easily reverts to an army state. Both faces are distinguishable only from the colours of their uniforms but in their primitiveness one.

It was the British colonial West African Frontier Force (WAFF) which provided the early military structure in the region. The WAFF soon metamorphosed into the local armies of the former British colonies. If other countries succeeded in reforming and civilising the colonial army and the internal security systems of the police, this was not so for Nigeria whose leaders have continued to thrive under the same abuses that sustained and preserved the colonial status quo. Consequently the police are constituted to serve the interests of a corrupt executive, perpetuate the latter's hold on power for as long as the system lasts, and use all available machinery to quell civil uprising and intimidate opposition. Because it is an unimaginative institution, being run in the monstrous hierarchy of its executive manipulators, its exploit in politics was already a foregone conclusion at the hands of successively crooked establishments in the country. The unbridled venality of the entire police rank and file seems their price for returning the federal and state executives to their power stools by mindless rigging of elections. And when their inefficiency in coping with civil unrest grows intolerable, the army is invited to assist in the objective of internal subjugation.

The number of checkpoints on highways and city corners, with their vile conduct attests to the connivance of the highest echelons that benefit from the activities of this morally reprehensible assemblage of men in uniform. Four politically emasculated states of the east, namely: Enugu, Anambra, Imo and Abia have succumbed to the coercion and blackmail of the populace by police - all geared to extend the comfort zones of those in power. The federal executives are all aware of the excesses of these men in dark regalia but the crimes of Nigeria Police are crimes against civil society so they look the other way.

Unfortunately, nowhere in the history of Nigeria's mendacious governments have police unmasked crimes perpetrated from echelons of executive office. Two poignant cases out of the plethora of orchestrated assassinations will suffice: The murder of Nigerian journalist and media proprietor, Dele Giwa, in 1987, described as gruesome and barbaric, has never been uncovered by the police even when the instrument of dispatch, a parcel bomb, was easily traced to military intelligence in General Ibrahim Babangida's junta. The recent political murder of Nigeria's justice minister, Bola Ige, mildly deemed embarrassing to government, has not been resolved by the PDP-led 'democratic' regime under whose watch the crime took place. This constitutes more than an outrage considering the 'anti corruption' posture of this government. Yet the executive that presides over the state of affairs has not seen this failure as its own. Successive governments will carry on even more comfortably in their fortified Aso Rock State house. Always it is 'business as usual', a sort of administrative amnesia that precludes any possibility of righting wrongs or learning from past mistakes except where it comes to dispatching their enemies with the active or conniving support of state security.

In addition to political murders are crimes that take place in the midst of incessant checkpoints on roads where police have the most visibility. Daily ordinary people are subjected to harassment, extortion and murderous robbery by men supposed to protect them. It is the only country in the world where police kills for mere twenty-Naira bribe. Nigerian writing is replete with gruesome details of such notoriety at checkpoints, an activity that qualifies in any civilised society as pure banditry:

> The police sergeant was dragging her in the direction of a small cluster of round huts not far from the road and surrounded as was common in these parts by a fence of hideously-spiked cactus. He was pulling her by the wrists, his gun slung from his shoulder. A few of the passengers mostly other women were pleading and protesting timorously. But most of the men found it very funny indeed. She threw herself down on her buttocks in desperation. But the sergeant would not let up. He dragged her along on the seat of her once neat blue dress through clumps of scorched tares and dangers of broken glass. (*Anthills* 215)

Now if any reader should think this incredible in a modern nation, how about the ensuing event, utterly larger-than-life, as a Nigerian reality:

> Chris bounded forward and held the man's hand and ordered him to release the girl at once. As if that was not enough he said, 'I will make a report about this to the Inspector-General of Police.'

'You go report me for where? You de craze! No be you de ask about President just now? If you no commot for my front now I go blow your head to Jericho, craze man.'

'Na you de craze,' said Chris. 'A police officer stealing a load of beer and then abducting a school girl! You are a disgrace to the force.'

The other said nothing more. He unslung his gun, cocked it, narrowed his eyes while confused voices went up all around some asking Chris to run, others the policeman to put the gun away. Chris stood his ground looking straight into the man's face, daring him to shoot. And he did, point blank into the chest presented him. (216)

To such atrocities by Nigerian men in uniform as presented in this account government response is usually apologetic and cosmetic. It will proffer occasional stylish raids by a 'task-force' (a term still prevalent in democracy) to bring few culprits to book. These tokens, borne from the usual backward approach to problem solving, appeal greatly to the psyche of leaders and citizens. Within the system, the victims are the unprotected ranks - unprotected, that is, from the nepotism of the godfathers. Nepotism is the rule of thumb that guarantees any reward or career prospect in Nigeria's entire public organization.

A Bleak Vision of the Civil State

Postcolonial Nigeria is bogged by the fraud that engineered it from the beginning. The ingenious British scheme of handing over in a controversy of number and geography to a northern oligarchy that would be convenient to manipulate played itself out to the full detriment of the Nigerian state. CODESRIA researchers state:

The colonial powers with the aid of missionary-anthropologists attributed characteristics to different groups that corresponded to

24

their fantastic imagination, classifying some as 'courageous'', "gallant", "resourceful' and "trustworthy" and others as "cowardly", "unreliable", "rebellious", and "crafty" and setting them on the part of conflictual, zero-sum competition. (2005)

After colonial Britain left behind the security apparatus that enforced its divide-and-rule policy with coercive taxes, the new locals inherited and added their own recipe of ethnicity and pseudo-nationalistic pretensions. Nigeria's Tafawa Balewa at independence banquet was proud to have the British first as masters, now as friends. But in their 1776 declaration of independence over two centuries ago the United States had preferred to treat their colonial masters as enemies in war:

We must endeavor to forget our former love for them, and hold them as we hold the rest of mankind, enemies in war... Therefore we the representatives of the United States of America in General Congress assembled, do in the name, and by the authority of the good people of these states reject and renounce all allegiance and subjection to the kings of Great Britain and all others who may hereafter claim by through or under them; we utterly dissolve all political connection which may heretofore have subsisted between us and the people or parliament of Great Britain: and finally we do assert and declare these colonies to be free... And for the support of this declaration, we mutually pledge to each other our lives, our fortunes, and our sacred honor. (Oxford 11)

The newly independent Nigerian elite who walked into the offices of their past masters and acclimatized to the status quo so thoroughly enjoyed the colonial largesse and subjugated their own people that the only difference lay in their barbarity. Onwubiko tells how during the Aba women's riot of 1929-1930, troops were called in to help the police in quelling the disturbances and, in the process, fifty unarmed women were killed (263). Now this, or even the Coal Miners revolt in

Enugu, was nothing in cruelty and executive mindlessness with Nigeria's recent example seventy years later in the Odi massacre of 2003. While the colonial police killed fifty unarmed women, President Obasanjo's army decimated a whole village of men, women, children and livestock.

For all its size and nature's endowments Nigeria's image remains unflattering. Tourism is virtually non-existent. Foreign visitors would be smart to prefer countries like Ghana, Cote d'Ivoire or even Cameroon to a nightmarish venture in Nigeria. It has been noted that the single most corrupt institution in the country is the police. But this is probably one country in the world where senators, assemblymen and presidents share the national loot in large fibre-woven bags errantly dubbed 'Ghana-must-go' - in reference to the expulsion of West African nationals from the country by the inept 1980s administration of Shehu Shagari. Ironically, it is the turn of Nigeria's unemployed youths to migrate to neighbouring countries as prostitutes and petty fraudsters. While the Black Star nation had recorded some success in its clean-up restoration of the state and the unification of its nationalities only by the exemplary leadership of Rawlings and his team, the Giant of Africa records majestic failure in any rehabilitation effort due to the serial fraudulence of its leaders since independence. The political lesson it did not learn from Ghana (preferring deceitful and empty boasts) was that no leadership succeeds with the predacious mentality that precipitates eventual downfall. At the height of the Buhari revolution of 1985, with their ludicrous claim to links with the preceding Murtala misadventure in politics, the poet Niyi Osundare warns:

A horseman gallops to power/ And tyrants of all the world rejoice/ Torture chambers multiply apace/ And the noose thickens,

26

descending/ A new horseman/ With guns in the saddle/ One for
dissidents at home/ Another for maddening rivals/ In the land of the
rising sun/ A new horseman/ With trust in might/ He will build
arsenals/ In place of barns/ And prod the poor/ To gorge on bullets.
(45)

The warning is echoed by many younger poets of the new
tradition. A poem on Obasanjo's ascension to the presidency in
1999 haunts us with its contempt for a fraudulent political
arrangement that was masked under the euphoria of
democracy:

A sluggard has slouched/ His paunches/ On to Aso Rock/ To smear
the palace sides/ With his sloven mirth…It is kakistocracy day/ And
he makes klieg lights/ Of minds cracked/ With the disease of road
blindness/ What future curse of the/ Triangle/ Awaits our children,
folks,/ If you let him. (*Eclipse* 12)

Regrettably the overawed masses of Nigeria seem to pitch
their tents with the same elements that unleash this running
spate of havoc in their lives. One of their popular slogans is
'You chop, I chop,' a euphemism for public corruption. This is
how the undiscerning elite celebrate democracy as tutored by
the regime that cancelled the only election deemed most free
and fair in 1993 and nearly embroiled the country in war.
Similarly, beneficiaries of the current dividends of serial
corruption are ardent for their men to retain the power
showcase at next elections. This is imperative for them
considering how easily they squander their loot round about
Europe, all round the hey-days of the military, and on to the
present civilian debacle. Evidently the insane elite in politics
do not care about a revolution. They know that Nigerian
masses are not cut in the cloak of their French counterparts but

will remain content with their own men in government - the cronyism that seems the fast lane to covetous loots.

It will dishearten any reader that while Nigerian literature has continued to flourish with the elegant promise of their brightest minds, the country is awkwardly positioned as the modern scourge of Africa thanks to her political leaders. That Nigeria is far from becoming a nation in the millennium is not in doubt. It is a country ruled by illiterate men - illiteracy in Fowler's terms 'being not simply one who cannot read and write but one who is unacquainted with good literature' (*Creation* 19).

There is one question that the bards have posed to present and past leaders jostling to return and continue the pillage where they left off: Whatever happened to all those promises of 'Health for all by Year 2000', 'Potable water for all by Year 2000', 'Housing for all by Year 2000'? It is a question none of them would vouchsafe to answer. In tourism Nigeria will remain the white and black man's grave. Its natural endowments which ought to make it great by sound management are tainted with neglect by lying and stealing governments, urban environments that qualify for health hazards, and public systems manipulated to swindle foreigners and locals alike. Time-priced virtues of human trust, honour and service are taken as follies of gullibility; verbal agreements, even when they are subject to written verification, are easily violated because the legal jurisdictions are capable of being bought and corrupted. Soyinka portrays the scenario so aptly in Beatification:

SANDA...Come, sir. I have an idea. (He takes BIG MAN SHOPPER aside.) Yes, sir, you are right, we could go to the police. BIG MAN SHOPPER Let's do that right away. We've lost too much time already.

SANDA. But then again, sir, you know what the police are like. (BIG MAN SHOPPER becomes instantly crestfallen.) Yes, sir, I am glad to see you do. He's only small fry, and his real bosses will simply come and bail him out, and that's the last you will see of him, and your missing valuables. The police will take their money and forget you.

BIG MAN SHOPPER (sighs). I have documents in that suitcase. Even my passport. The money doesn't matter so much, but I have important business papers...(43)

There are countless signposts from the writings of Nigeria's talented poets and novelists; their voices trail the frightful carnage of the civil war, the foolish extravaganzas of the seventies, the miseries of the eighties, the nightmares of the nineties and the present buffoonery of the millennium. Nigerian fiction and non-fiction writers agree with one voice that her political future is doomed by a handful that refresh themselves in endless rounds of military and civilian misgovernment with their trump cards set to buy the last vestige of public conscience. We have seen evidence that government educational policy, or lack of it, can only guarantee the continued production of ignoramuses for leaders. Obviously then the singsong about 'labours of heroes past' is suspect when real evidence of transition from education-for-white-collar-jobs to functional literacy is non-existent forty years after. This condition can only lead to disaster in all democratic experiments. It appears that the country will be bedridden with this affliction for a very long time. As a ship with a confraternity of pirates at the helm, Nigeria is set to wobble abysmally in darkness until natural cataclysms hasten its disintegration where the degenerate crew would have led it in the first place.

Until then, in the short run perhaps, Africans may just have to pray for their big-for-nothing brother along the lines of one of Nigeria's new female poets:

Say to us/ Desolation shall no longer marry this land/ Every ruler-thief shall be/ Burned as fuel for the fire/ My vow shall entwine its roots deep in truth/ And bear a sheltering nest, your great reward/ You'll dare again to nurse the eggs of hope/ Trusting the chicks shall not be scrap metal. (Adewale 64)

Approaches

Chapter Two

Africa in the Narratives of Laurence

P.Ugor

Africa, quite simply to Margaret Laurence, meant coming home to Canada (Tapping 73).

The Foreign Novel of Africa: An Introduction

AFRICA continues to feature in global discourses whether in the realm of politics, culture, economics, and religion or other universal issues of human interests. These growing interests in the continent derives perhaps from its peculiar history as one recovering from prolonged imperial conquest from Europe and the Americas, and its purported backwardness in the context of western civilization. The attention on the continent therefore arises not only from the routine surveillance of a deterritorialized globe (by enduring imperial powers) welded together by science and technology, but also by an imperative to apprehend the life of the people thereof. In this regard, the cultural sector, both of the First World and Developing Nations, has played a significant role. In the literary circuit for example there exist a rich oeuvre of literary pieces both from within and outside the continent that have tried to privilege insights into the people and their ways. In this context, what Michael Echeruo has referred to as the "Foreign Novel of Africa" has had a significant place and impact. This phrase has come to refer to that large body of narratologies by western writers set in Africa and contoured by a narrative tradition in which "the narrative prejudice is more important than the narrated fact"[1].

Indeed, it is imperative to trace the genealogy of this narrative genre. Beginning from the 16th century the whole of Europe was at its feverish peak of conquering lands and people beyond its shores. The declaration of a German scholar, Von Trieschke, published in 1914, effectively captures the prevailing mentality of the whole of Europe at the time. And we have elected to call attention to the statement because it provides insights into the popular inclinations in Europe that inadvertently led to the emergence of the novel of Africa by the west. According to Trieschke

> Today we see the nations of Europe busily engaged in creating all over the globe a wholesale aristocracy of the white race. That nation which does not take a share in this great rivalry will play a pitiful part at some later day. It is therefore a vital question for a great nation today to display a craving for colonies. (Henderson 31).

The growing industrial capitalism in the west necessitated enormous raw materials and human capital in the form of labour. Owing to these needs, navigation and trade became the noblest foundations of any European state. Firm optimistic reports from explorers, traders and missionaries of the economic viabilities of various parts of Africa and the Pacific became alluring bait for the west that was in dire need of raw materials for its growing industries. Africa thus became a strong attraction for countries such as Britain, France, Germany, Portugal, Belgium, etc. Expectedly, a flood of young men and women from the west made incursions into the continent as colonial administrators, company representatives, traders, military

33

personnel, sailors, and in other different imperialist capacities.

But the conquered territories were not only an outpost of economic progress for Europe but also an outpost of "literary progress". Uprooted from a different cultural universe, these teeming crowd of young westerners were however unprepared for the cultural disparities they were to encounter in the different African countries they were deployed to. The result was not only culture shock but also fierce conflicts between colonial authorities and indigenous peoples. On returning home these experiences served as grist for a new kind of narrative for the reading public of the whole of Europe and the Americas, which at the time were in search of the exotic in narrative texture. Colonial agents such as Mongo Park, Joyce Cary, Joseph Conrad and a host of others wrote creative pieces fertilized by their experiences in the course of their trips. In fact, Conrad was acclaimed in the west as one of the finest writers "of western civilization"(Watts xxiii). He wrote amongst many others *Heart of Darkness* (1899) and *An Outpost of Progress* (1898) while Cary wrote Mr. Johnson. Some of these literary accounts were even produced as films at later dates. These cultural texts were representative of what the west had to say about "places out on the frontiers where European civilization extended its imperial arms" (Hammer ix). Taken together, these creative pieces "brought to life for European readers alien environments that few could ever know personally" (Hammer 1). But they also generated debates as to whether the stories did not "exploit natives as pawns against exotic backdrops for the dramatization of European concerns" (2).

Indeed it was these concerns that catalyzed the evolution of African literature. Pioneer African writers who themselves had attended colonial institutions such as missionary schools and satellites of western universities in the colony or in the west were thoroughly tutored in western curriculum so they had exposure to the various writings of Africa by the west. Their writings therefore started as textual oppositions to these jaundiced narratives. Foremost African writers such as Chinua Achebe or Wole Soyinka have confessed that some of their writings were indeed actuated by the longing to respond to some novelists of Africa such as Conrad and Cary.

It is important to ask what these writings meant and implied as cultural expressions. This question has become imperative in the context of our concern of the field of cultural production and the power currents that shape and influence the construction of culture. Within this critical purview, "the practice of criticism, consequently, is not limited to the immediate analysis of the work in question but it also involves a telling-over of the powers latent in the language"(Walsh 9). In other words we construe culture as a textual power rhetoric propelled by invisible political forces that imbue them with a certain kind of clout; cultural capital. Chinua Achebe, novelist, poet and scholar has advanced a convincing logic in apprehending the "Novel of Africa" as cultural capital. In his paper entitled "An Image of Africa", Achebe critiques Conrad's *Heart of Darkness*, describing the author and the novel " racist"(8). According to Achebe Conrad and his like were "purveyors of comforting myths" which satisfied the desire in "western psychology to set Africa up as a foil in Europe, a place of negations at once remote and vaguely familiar in comparison with which Europe's own state of spiritual grace will be manifest"(3). Consistently then, these narratives portray Africa as primordial jungles, barbaric and still in a state of nature's harmony unlike Europe's civilized social space. As Achebe has noted, the likes of Conrad did not originate those images of Africa for they were already dominant perceptions in western imagination. But such literary fantasies had important socio- cultural ramifications. According to him

> The west seems to suffer deep anxieties about the precariousness of its civilization and to have a need for constant reassurance by comparing it with Africa. If Europe, advancing in civilization, could cast a backward glance periodically at Africa trapped in primordial barbarity, it could say with faith and feeling: There go I but for the grace of God. Africa is to Europe as the picture is to Dorian Grey -a carrier onto whom the master unloads his physical and moral deformities so that he may go forward, erect and immaculate. (Achebe 17)

This superb logic of the cultural politics behind the "Novel of Africa" makes profound sense when cast against the social and political context in which that narrative genre emerged in Europe. The last late nineteenth century "was a time of imperialistic fervour in Britain" where the reign of queen Victoria extolled "the growth of British economic power, military strength and territory" (Watts viii). The foreign narratives of Africa were therefore cultural symbols of western cultural, social, political, economic and religious superiority played against the canvass of recognizable backward peoples. For a long time, the reading public of the west was inundated with these literary staple and they have continued to manifest in other aspects of western life in very congealed ways.

Strangely however, especially beginning from the mid-twentieth century in North America, some western writers radically departed from the familiar tale of Africa where barbarism is routinely juxtaposed with western civilization. A good example is Canadian writer Margaret Laurence. According to Douglas Killam, "we get a convincing, rounded, intelligent and sympathetic experience of the life of Africans in African community; how Africans think and feel, what their lives really mean, how their beliefs really function" (x-xi). Unlike her western predecessors therefore, her narratives are a more benign and humane portrayal of Africa. This is indeed a curious departure from a long and encrusted western literary tradition and it is perhaps appropriate to interrogate and rethink the factors that have accounted for this narrative deviation. What we see in these narratives is a unique literary technique wherein Laurence deploys the social space of Africa as a stage for imagining cross-cultural interaction in Canada for her own nationalist purposes. In other words, we do not counteract the popular perception of her works as humanizing Africa but that this authentic image of Africa is to an end; that of forging Canadian multi-culturalism as begun in the 1950s.

Margaret Laurence: A Biographic Insight

Of Scottish ancestry, Margaret Laurence was born as Margaret Wemyss to Robert Wemyss and Verna Simpson on 18th July, 1926 in Neepawa, Manitoba, Canada. Her early life is somewhat tumultuous as she lost her mother at the tender age of four, was nurtured by her aunt who later married her father and grew up in an austere neighborhood marked by a strained relationship between her grandparents. These early family tumults seem to have molded a deeply meditative character within Laurence that led to her writing career in later life. At age eighteen she gained admission to Winnipeg's United College, an affiliate of the University of Manitoba where she took an honors degree in English in 1947. There, she demonstrated her writing aptitude right from her undergraduate days publishing items in the student's magazine. Working briefly after graduation as a reporter, she married Jack Laurence, a civil engineer graduate from the University of Manitoba. This marriage was to set her life on the path of creative writing beginning with her trip to British Somali-land protectorate (now Somalia) and the Gold coast (now Ghana) in Africa between 1950- 1957 with her husband who was on a Dam-building assignment. According to Clara Thomas "when Margaret reminisced with me about her African years, it was almost always about the books that had issued from them and her admiration for African people and their ancient tribal cultures" (265). Margaret Laurence's African experiences did not only incense her creative impulses but they also honed them for it was there that she began and perfected her creative talents. For as she acknowledged herself "it really was Africa which taught me to look at myself" (Quoted in Xiques 7).

Her corpus, including essays, fiction, autobiography, translations and fiction for young adults set in both Africa and Canada amount to about fifteen in number. Here we are however restricted to her African writing alone. They include *A Tree for Poverty* (1954); *This Side Jordan* (1960); *The Tomorrow-Tamer* (1963); *The Prophet Camel Bell* (1963); and a book of critical essays on Nigerian writers: *Long Drums and Cannons: Nigerian Dramatists and Novelists 1952-1966* (1966). Taken together, these rich oeuvre addressed themes of exile, faith, love, the journey towards wholeness, personhood, the drive to freedom, the unique dignity of every individual, loss, despair, anxiety (Thomas 266-67) and many more human emotions experienced by both Africans and non-Africans brought together by the accident of history. Her ability to churn out these large body of creative pieces set in Africa, a feat not accomplished by some of the African scholars and creative writers tucked away in Africa's educational and cultural institutions, is a great testimony to her love for the places she made forays into in the course of her sojourn on the continent. In this regard, referring to her specific Somaliland context, Donez Xiques has noted that "Margaret Laurence' love for the Somaliland (African) culture and religion was in sharp contrast to the negative attitudes and the strong sense of superiority then common among many of the British in the protectorate" (9). It is perhaps no wonder that her narrative style and treatment of content differed radically from other western writers of Africa discussed earlier on in the introduction. It is perhaps interesting and imperative then to investigate this literary style evolved by Margaret Laurence in making sense of it as a distinct cultural capital. That is, one imbued with a new cultural symmetry with the purpose of speaking to an existing asymmetrical power set up.

Why should we pay attention to Margaret's African writings in the context of a topic that seems essentially Canadian? It is perhaps because recent theoretical trends in literary studies the worlds over have shifted attention to what has been referred to as the "post- colonial condition"; one which Canada is thoroughly implicated in and consciously and vigorously grappling with. Citing Patrick Williams and Laura Chrisman, Christian Riegel has noted that the dislodgement of colonialism is "one of the most spectacular events or series of events of the 20th century". He then argues that "if we stake any validity to that claim in the least- and the growing body of theory that examines post-coloniality seems to support such claims- then we must pay more attention to a writer such as Laurence in that context"(xiv). The appropriate place to begin then is her African narratives for it is there that the tension that pervades decolonizing entities is aptly narrativised. *This Side Jordan*, Laurence's first novel (which is also considered as her *Magnus Opus*), for which this study is largely based and her other African writings foreground what Mary Rimmer has referred to as "personal and cultural power struggles"(4), in what Bourdieu (1993) calls "The Field of Cultural Production". According to Gabrielle Collu *This Side Jordan* best "illustrates well what we mean by representing the other, land and people, within an awareness of the power dynamics inevitable in representation together with the cultural differences involved, and particularly with exemplary empathy and humility"(20).

Laurence's African Narratives

Margaret Laurence began her African narratives in the 1950s. This period is indeed significant if we recognize the shared cultural consciousness and concerns that the continent of Africa, especially Ghana where she was domiciled, had in common with Canada where she hails from. After decades of imperialism by Europe, the whole of the continent of Africa was agog with nationalistic zeal and the quest for independence was at a fierce peak. This nationalistic tempo permeated all frontiers- political, cultural, economic, social, religious and more. It was a defining moment of the search for identity and freedom in the African colonies. But this sense of nationalism was not new as it was ongoing in other Commonwealth States but perhaps in other ways and forms. Canada had been colonized by Britain, secured its own freedom, participated in the two world wars, and was frantically trying to evolve her own distinct political and cultural identity from its colonizers and the tide of American cultural flood. For both Ghana and Canada as nations then, it was a period of becoming; of defining nationhood on all fronts, and the cultural sector had a significant place in this national agenda. Also, as Canada was a shaped by multicultural diversity, so was Africa a medley of cultural elements (Europeans, Americans, Asians) coalesced together by a sordid history. The vagaries of post-coloniality were thus a shared travail between both national entities. An observable eye, the young Laurence never missed capturing the drama unfolding before her; a cultural episode that struck familiar chords from home in Canada. In her own words: "it was not very difficult to relate this experiences to my own land, which had been under the colonial sway of Britain once and was now under the colonial sway of America" (Quoted in Barbara Pell 36). When she began cataloguing the cultural crisis playing out before her it was with sensitivity to the cultural needs of her own home country. When she wrought her African works then, it served as a cultural and political paradigm for the handling of the similar experiences that her country was undergoing at the time. Christian Riegel affirms this much when he wrote that Margaret's writings "spoke to the new sense of cultural nationalism that Canada was experiencing in the late 1960s and the early 1970s...she provided a body of work that fulfilled a need by a Canadian public eager to explore their own identity- their own psychic space"(xii). Similar to the literary pieces of indigenous African writers, Laurence's African writings worked "to illuminate a period of history and to communicate an understanding gained from contemplating it". Only that "Margaret Laurence was in tune with the times when she wrote than she new" (Killam xii).

In doing this, the city became an inevitable narrative locale for her writings. *This Side Jordan* and most of her African corpus is set in the contemporary African cities of the 1950s. The African cities bear the scars of imperialism most and it is there too that the quest for freedom; both political and cultural, plays out. As Kenneth Little had noted "it is the city that provides the best guides to the current social attitudes and trends. It is there that the major decisions are made, that social change is most rapid" (2). It is in the urbanity of the city space that the miasma of contemporary existence is best glimpsed; where the forces of modernity and indigenous or local logic collide. It is in the African cities that the cultural anxieties that plagued Canada were better visualized and captured for a nation desperately in search of her own cultural identity. The African city, that vast field of culture provided a wide view of how other peoples were mapping their own cultural terrain. It was indeed a lofty human episode in cultural engineering for Canada to see and forge its way through the cultural maze without stumbling on the impediments that the writer saw in other lands.

When the novel opens, a sharp binary of cultural tension is immediately epitomized in the divided perception of the dance between Johnnie Kestoe and Charity at the nightclub called "Weekend in Wyoming". The following lines from the novel captures the immediate spirit of hate, suspicion and distrust between blacks and whites that pervades the atmosphere: "At one of the tables around the outdoor dance floor, a young European woman watched thoughtfully. At another table an African man watched, then turned away and spat. Both were angry and with the same person" (*Jordan* 1). It is the comments that follow what seems an innocuous social pastime that leads us to the inner workings of the two communities set up for us in the novel: blacks and whites. The small group of whites in the bar is made up of James Bedford and his wife, Cora Thayer, and Johnnie and Miranda Kestoe. The comments that precede Johnnie's dance (with an African girl) from that group show a deep sense of resentment and near disgust that the small white community has against the blacks. Victor's reproach of Charity on the other hand also tells of a deep sense of hate for the whites. In between this deep divide is Miranda Kestoe who provides a mediating force throughout the story. In all, this opening narrates the attitude of the tiny white middle class to the blacks and the corresponding hate of the blacks symbolized in Victor Edusei. But this division that Margaret creates for us is not new for even in Canada at the time a fierce rivalry and deep resentment existed between First Nations peoples (as well as other minority population such as Asians, Hispanics and Africans) and the settler European population. How the African example was going to be reconciled was going to be an instructive example in engineering multiculturalism.

Central in the whole narrative is Nathaniel. It is through his character that we gain insight into the inner crisis of the colonial subject. In many ways he is half-baked: he has incomplete education as he didn't pass even high school final exams; he is torn between a nostalgia for a traditional African past and the allure of modernity (the city); he straddles between African traditional belief and Christian values and, confused between moral principles and the dictates of survivalism in the urban colony. According to Clara Thomas, "Nathaniel is caught...in a strangling web of circumstances whose threads were tangled and noted by himself, by others and by the impersonal but inexorable march of history itself" (102). Nathaniel is a quintessential example of the colonial African torn between two cultural worlds. This character of the colonial African is itself steeped in a long history. The early Europeans who made incursions into Africa sought to make an Englishman out of the African by not only Christianizing their souls and resacralizing their social space but also by imparting British middle-class etiquettes. Schools, which dispensed western education, became central to this cultural policy. But the colonial governments and the missionaries could only do enough as indigenous Africans had no financial capital to pursue higher education after the token of elementary western tutelage they got from missionary schools. The result was a large chunk of Africans prematurely ripped away from their traditional backgrounds and incompletely assimilated to western culture. Referring to this indeterminate position of the African in the novel Margaret writes in describing Nathaniel that "both gods had fought over him and both had lost" (*Jordan* 32). These Africans sought the tinsel of the modern world without the necessary credentials to participate in it and detested the African villages that beckoned them for service. Nathaniel neither could return to the village to serve his clan chief who desperately wanted his services nor secure a good paying job in Accra, the capital of Ghana. Gradually the forces of the modern world pushed and shoved him to moral degeneration; for he resorts to taking bribe from young school drop-outs he seeks to help with jobs at Johnnie Kestoe's company. Summarizing these problems the text comments "So many desires. Kumi and Awuletey's desire to have jobs that were big and important. Nathaniel's desire to create a place of belonging for those who had no place. The desire to do something, be somebody. The desire to be God and the desire to wear a silk shirt" (*Jordan* 208). It was a torrent of desires indeed. It is important to note that this crisis of two cultural worlds was not unfamiliar to Laurence. In Canada, the systematic policies drawn to make Europeans of First Nations peoples through residential schools and foster homes in what has come to be known as the "the 60s scoops" and the disastrous psychological and cultural outcome of such cultural superimposition was perhaps still ingrained in her cultural memory. Suzanne Fournier and Ernie Crey have eloquently demonstrated this in their book *Stolen From Our Embrace: the Abduction of First Nations Children and the Restoration of Aboriginal Communities. Africa* only enabled Laurence see this cultural tragedy from a privileged position. At a time when Canada was jittery about managing its diversity into a uniform whole, Laurence's writings seem to have been illustrating Robert England's warnings "that the type of social life to which a race has accustomed itself must be touched with care..."(quoted in Day 156). It was a reaffirmation of the view that an integrating cultural policy with "a more subtle form, in which the preservation of certain signs of otherness was seen as permissible, perhaps even more desirable" (Day 165) was a less disastrous way to go.

If Nathaniel is a metaphor for the whirling currents that besiege the colonial struggling with social change around him, Margaret also narrativizes the anxieties of the colonizing force. With the upsurge in nationalism, especially political activism in the colonies in quest of independence, the economic policies of the ruling imperialist had to be adapted to suit the prevailing moments and to accommodate the emerging black power elites. Inevitably, the power structure among the tiny white middle- class had to be shaken. This impending upstaging of the hierarchy amongst the privileged European working class in the colony portended personal disaster for they existed amongst these whites their own "Nathaniels"; people like Johnnie Kestoe and the Bedfords who are actually never-do-wells from their home country but have made it big in the colonies due to the color of their skin. Bedford's wife tells Johnnie "Do I tell you why we can't go back to England?...It's because Bedford can't get a job there. He can do a little of everything and not enough of everything" (*Jordan* 123). Laurence herself has provided vivid examples from her experience in Somali in her travel diary *The Prophet's Camel Bell*. In it she refers to people who were so desperately uncertain of their own worth and their abilities to cope within their own societies that there were forced to seek some kind of mastery in a place where all the cards were stacked in their favor and where they could live in a self-generated glory by transferring all evils, all weaknesses, on to another people (quoted in Githae-Mugo,11).

She has also reiterated this point in her interview with Rosemary Sullivan in a book of essays by and about her entitled *A place to Stand On* (67). The great anxiety and panic around the tiny European working class in Allkirk, Moore and Bright Company was truly founded on this fear. Africanization meant that prime managerial positions were going to be taken from whites and given to blacks as independence approached. It is not so much the antics of survival and betrayals between Johnnie and other white staff that interest me in the context of our study. Rather, it is the clue it gives us into the discomfort that radical changes bring to any society. The managers in Moore and Bright are reluctant to cede the economic power that they have enjoyed for many years to the new dispensation of Africanization. This reluctance throws a significant sidelight on the nature of people; what culture, a way of life means to people and how difficult it is to give it up. Giving up positions is like giving up culture. What Margaret does with the Africanization subplot is to make those who wish to coerce change in people taste and feel what change entails. When those who seek change are made to taste it, the perception of it differs. This insight into the nature of change was an edifying example of the painful realities of cultural transitions. No nation needed this wise lesson more than Canada, which was refashioning its cultural self in the 1950s, when Margaret Laurence was writing. Within this logic it is important to call attention to the post-writing adjustments that took place with the novel. Margaret herself had confessed: "I had already written half the book from scratch when I decided, after leaving Africa and getting a fresh perspective on colonial society, that I'd been unfair to the European characters" (Ten Years Sentence 28). But it was not only the fresh "perspective" on otherness alone. The publishers, McClelland and Stewart, were also asking for a tinkering of the European characters perhaps as courtesy to the European readers. What this points at clearly is that both the author and the publishing company as literary institutions knew that though the novel was about Africa, Laurence was not writing for Africans but for Europeans and Canadians. If she was to speak to her audience effectively about the dangers of coercive integrative cultural policies (which the Canadian government was unwinding at the time), she needed to strike a delicate balance between the two cultural entities or forces; European and others. She needed to portray culture in dialogue during a process of change rather than taking sides or What Robert Lecker has described as "shareability and the 'strategy of containment" (n.p). By hearkening to the request by the publishers, Laurence was conforming to the prevailing literary canon.

This narrative equity that Margaret displays has unique import for the position being articulated here. By narrative equity one is referring to the manner in which key characters in both sides of the cultural divide are portrayed. They are apportioned blame and absolved of mistakes equitably. Here the characters of Johnnie Kestoe and Nathaniel come to mind. From the outset we get a condescending impression towards Africans by Johnnie Kestoe. But beneath that facade of detestation is a lingering desire for black women; "You English- you want to try a black girl, see what she's like. But all very quiet and secret" says Saleh (Jordan 88). He is a hard working, honest professional and good husband. But he also seeks the pleasure of black whores outside of his marital home. Not only does he show lascivious traits when he visits Saleh's shop and sees his sexy daughter but actually patronizes an African girl on her first time out in a night club; an encounter which leads to the reopening of the girl's clitoridectomy scar. This erotic encounter has been conceived in both literal and metaphorical terms. Mary Rimmer for instance has argued "seeking a stereotypical encounter with Africa, Johnnie thinks of Emerald as 'continent' and of himself as 'an invader, wanting both to posses and to destroy" (12).

We are however more interested in what this complicity in extra- marital relationship tells about the character of Johnnie than its larger textual interpretation. It points us to his personal weaknesses as a personality just as Nathaniel's acceptance of a token from the two school leavers tell us of his own character flaw. Together both possess weaknesses and strengths, which is human and which society ought to acknowledge, respect and manage. What does this tell us about the home of the author? The stories of foster parents or masters who had sexual relationships with indigenous peoples in their care (whether forceful or consensual) abound here (see Fournier and Crey). The incorrigible alcoholism of First Nations people on the other hand can also be seen as their own flaw. What is central to the portrayal of these weaknesses on either side of the cultural divide is to call attention to the need for tolerance where people's differences and strengths are maximized for the collective good of society rather than out right dismissal as never-do-wells. It was a huge lesson in managing differences; a cultural policy Canada espoused at the time (see Day's "The Rise of the Mosaic Metaphor").

The novel ends on a note of hope; one which Laurence herself became doubtful of many years after. She voiced this pessimism in her essay "Ten Year Sentences". But it is important to call attention to the role of Miranda (Kestoe's wife) in this projected change. From the beginning of the novel to its end, Miranda plays a mitigating role to the tensed nerves in the narrative symbolized by the strained relationship between Johnnie and Nathaniel. She functions as a conveyor-belt negotiating alliances between two opposing cultural and ideological poles. Her role may smack of a survivalist trump card but it is through her that the dawn of mutual interdependence in an atmosphere of diversity is achieved. Victor Adesui (an African and London school of Economics post- graduate) is finally co-opted to work in Moore and Bright as assistant manager while Johnnie is retained as an accountant in spite of the Africanization policy; both sides "finally come to accept the reality and integrity of the other" (Pell 42). A new union amidst differences is forged and the future is assured. This future is symbolized by the newborn babies by both Nathaniel's wife (Aya) and Johnnie's Miranda. Both women are "equally heroic figures who become a bridge between the old and the new Africa" (Pell 42). A great hope for a potential mosaic land is metaphorical semiotized here. The least doubt is left for anyone aware of Canada's quest for a prosperous and successful multi cultural state that this was a great lesson in cultural engineering for the author's homeland. Nora Stovel, a Canadian and thorough going scholar of Margaret Laurence has affirmed this fact when she quoted Clara Thomas thus:

> Laurence's 'experiences of Africa issued in works that explored themes of exile, loss and mankind's stubborn, valiant quest for home and freedom; they also led her to see that these themes were particularly urgent to her own people as well.(Stovel xviii)

Perhaps it is also important to call attention to Laurence's other African writings that speak to the arguments we articulate in this work. Very significant is her collection of short stories *The Tomorrow-Tamer* first published in 1963 by Macmillan and re- issued in paperback edition by McClelland and Stewart in 1970. The book is actually a collection of stories written by Laurence and published by the University of British Columbia journals such as *Prism, Queen's Quarterly* and the *Saturday Evening Post* between 1956 and 1963. Indeed, two of the short stories from this collection "The Tomorrow-Tamer" and "A Gourdful of Glory" were "awarded the University of Western Ontario President's Medal of Excellence"(Thomas xi). The implication of the two institutions (McClelland and University of West Ontario), in the promotion of this book set in far away Africa, is somewhat curious and provokes thoughts. McClelland and Stewart were at the very forefront of Canadian nationalism and the Universities were setting standards or canons of genuine Canadian literature at the time. Being Canadian was not enough recognition to receive the imprimatur of these regulating cultural institutions, which were, are a time hard-nosed seekers of Canadian "national self-consciousness" in literary productivities (Lecker N.P). It likely may have spoken to the needs of the country in some unique way.

"The Tomorrow-Tamer" is set in the small village of Owurasu in Ghana, where the colonial government has decided that a bridge be built to connect the village and the cost. Very likely, as it was wont to be, the colonial government had an economic interest in opening up inaccessible hinterlands in the colonies. "The government men who are greater than any chief" see this as an "honour for your small village", Badu, the interpreter for the European engineers, tells the chiefs (T.T). In the process, the sacred grove of Awura (the protector/guardian spirit) of the village will be destroyed; its once calm waters disturbed. What follows is a booming economy and seeming development for the village. As the narrator reports "Six bungalows, servants' quarters, latrines and a long line of labourer's huts began to take shape. The young men of Awurasa were paid for their work. The village had never seen so much cash money before" (T.T 90). Even Danquah who could never sell a crate of beer in six months was able to do so in two days. But beneath this facade of a bourgeoning economy lurks an impending disaster for the village; the gods whose grove has been desecrated are angry and set to unleash its anger. Furthermore, not only are strange men and ways introduced to the village, but even their daughters are getting pregnant by an unknown "spirit" (The European engineers). Before long the bridge claims its first victim, Kofi, who works as a mechanic hand in the construction site. A once peaceful village is thrown into chaos, mourning and eternal pain. The bridge that was meant to bring civilisation to the people is rather a bearer of tragedies. If this story registered nothing at least it made the point about cultural relativism. For what might seem great, beneficent and acceptable to a people may be malicious and dangerous to others. This was a crucial cultural insight into the cautious management of cultural differences in any multi-ethnic/cultural entity and no one needed this cultural didactism more than Canada at the time. The stories in the *Tomorrow-Tamer* collection illustrated the fact that no one culture is uniformly good for all man. As Matthew, a character in one of the stories, meditates: "My father thought he was bringing salvation to Africa. I do not know any longer what salvation is. I only know that one man cannot find it for another man, and one land cannot bring it to another" ("The Drummer of All the World" 1). Here probably lays the great admiration that earned

51

Margaret Laurence her laurels from the cultural institutions such as McClelland and even the Universities that were the vanguards of Canadian nationalism at the time: For the work espoused the very tenets of national ethos that government policy sought to implant at that moment in the nation's history.

Another "significant element in Laurence's long list of literary accomplishments" (Reigel xiii) is her critical book of essays on Nigerian literature *Long Drums and Cannons* published in 1968 by Macmillan. In many ways this can be considered the earliest poetics on African literature. For only until after the early 1970s did critical discourses framing theoretical positions in African literature from within and outside the continent emerge. This was indeed a crucial and invaluable contribution to African literature because even up until the late 1970s, there still existed strong cynicism in western literary and secular social circles about the existence and worth of African literature. Christian Reigel has also made the vital point that "while Nigerian literature did not need Margaret Laurence to exist, it was usefully served by her decision to take up the task of making it known to a larger audience" (xii). And in doing that she was established not only as a colonial writer but also a savvy post-colonial critic with a crucial "role as an observer of the changes that accompanied the shift from a colonial country to a post-colonial, ultimately independent...nation" (Reigel xii). This was a unique literary take that was not only relevant to Africa but also to other post-colonial national sovereignties such as Canada. It was a period in which Canada as a nation was emphatic about what Frye has described as "the obvious and unquenchable desire of the Canadian cultural public to identify itself through its literature" (Quoted in Lecker, np). *If A Tree For Poverty* portrayed how a people preserved their identity through oral literature, *Long Drums and Cannons* showed how nations entrapped in the post- colonial identity problems were re-inventing and forging a new and distinct cultural self through their literary culture. It is important to understand the context of literary production from Nigeria at this moment. Much of the early writings were actuated by the need to re-order a faulty portrayal by the west (Europe) of Africa. Achebe for instance has captured the spirit behind the African writer in those moments when he said that "The whole pattern of life demanded that you put in a word for your history, your tradition, your religion and so on" (Lindfors et al, 7). It was a crucial historical moment when African writers were bent on re-imaging, re-inventing and re-negotiating an African presence in the global marketplace of ideas whether cultural, political, economic, religious or otherwise. Laurence's critical insights into Nigerian literary culture were therefore an invitation "to the world to see that individual Nigerian experience in literature also represents universal human experience" (Stovel cited in Na'Allah, Lvi). It was indeed an invaluable cultural pedagogy for a nation like Canada, Laurence's home country, which was refashioning its national self through many policies including the literary/cultural.

It is perhaps pertinent to make clear at this point that in attempting to articulate a connection between Laurence's African writings and their cultural value to the author's home country, one is not ignorantly engaged in drawing a parallel between Canada and Africa. The two do not share the same history in many national facets. Rather, it is important to show how her African writings dovetailed with the immediate cultural pursuits of her country at a certain historical moment, and signaling why she gained so much acclaim (cultural

53

capital) in North America by writing about Africa. That historical moment is significant in apprehending the logic of this presentation.

Until the early 1960's, Canada still maintained a racist policy of immigration. It was not until 1962 that the current "universal and non-discriminatory (immigration) policy" in Canada was introduced (Dirk cited in Groening, 96). At this time, Canada was consciously forging a national culture that would speak to the world and its citizens about its new national status and ideological bent. The country had become a member of the league of "8", the leading countries in the world, and thus was enthusiastic about portraying itself as a repentant nation from racist inclinations joining the league of great nations. According to Laura Groening, The New Canadian Library under the leadership of Malcolm Ross "was working to foster a national imaginary well prepared to welcome such change in social policy. Each text was selected to maintain a balance of regional, and, by extension, ethnic diversity" (96). Laurence's African writings, which mostly were about blacks and whites in conflict, spoke to this new national policy of accommodating otherness. Her "works by implication...guides the reader to confront racism, rather than announcing the blindness of all imperialisms" (Tapping 77).

It is no wonder then that regulating cultural institutions such as publishing houses (example McClelland and Stewart), funding agencies and even universities (purveyors of the Canadian canon) embraced Laurence's works and literary persona. Robert Lecker has noted for example that the Canada's Council Block Grant, which was meant to support the publication of literary culture "intended to support books written by Canadian authors which make an original contribution to the development of Canadian culture and identity, and which add to an understanding of this country and its peoples or the issues confronting the nation"(448). The council was interested in authors who would "witness culture for the benefit of the Canadian public" (Lecker 499). Here lies the Canadianess of Laurence's African writings. Though about, and set in far away Africa, her corpus spoke to the world about the on- going socio-cultural bias of the new Canada and gestured Canadian citizens towards a new sense of acceptance of difference. Canada at this moment was always narrativised in a way that implied goodness. As cultural productions, Laurence's African works "exhibited Canadian sensibilities" and "experiences" (Friskney,35). This was a unique form of witnessing culture in other spaces and adapting it to a new national end; it was what Paul Hjartarson and Tracy #Kulba have aptly tagged "The Politics of Cultural Mediation": that sense in which "text and people move from one place to another and that they are moved and repositioned by forces beyond themselves" (xx).

In her book *Heart of a Stranger*, Laurence declared, "one thing I learned...was that my experiences of other countries probably taught me more about myself and even my own land than about anything else" (11). What she learned from Africa was the crucial role that writers have in building national culture and she shared this knowledge with her fellow countrymen. Laurence's was the case of "the gradual empowering of a personal voice which will come back to Canada and do, in her writing, what those voices she discusses in her criticism of African traditions do, and had done, for their culture and people" (Tapping, 67). Those engineering Canada's national culture at the time; publishers, universities, funding agencies, had seen far ahead the cultural insights that she provided for the new nation. Only she herself may not have known. Because her African works spoke to the contemporaneous cultural sensibilities of Canada at the time, and perhaps many years after, she remains a looming cultural star in Canada's literary firmament.

Chapter Three

The Literary Economy of Congo Diary

I.Bello-Kano

We must be several in order to write. (Derrida, *Writing and Difference* 226)

Introduction

WHEN Joseph Conrad arrived in the Congo on June 12th 1890, he began a diary[1] whose first entry was dated June 13th 1890. He spent six months there, having been employed by the Belgian Societé Anonyme pour le Commerce du Haut-Congo, a company with extensive interests in the Congo Free State and identified in the diary as "the Company". The diary records Conrad's 320-km trek on the coast from Boma to Matadi, and then to Kinsasha; and, spectacularly, his enchantment and disenchantment, in equal measure, with the material and human landscape. The diary is written in an elliptical style; it is episodic and structurally organized around the date entry (or a chronological narrative frame). Yet the most dominant feature of the diary is Conrad's disenchantment with the body of the Congo as both a material-landscape and human presence. It records scenes and moments of anguish, discomfort, sickness, physical and mental exhaustion, the horror and horrid smell of decomposing bodies, and the disquieting sights of "white men's graves".

Many Conrad scholars have traditionally seen the significance of the diary as the background to Conrad's short story, "An Outpost of Progress" (1897) and the novella, *Heart of Darkness* (1899), Marlow's fictional journey in the Congo (although the setting of the novella is not disclosed). (See, on this, Jean-Aubry Joseph Conrad in the Congo; Sherry, Conrad's Western World; Najder, Joseph Conrad; Hampson, Joseph Conrad; Hawkins, "Conrad and Congolese Exploitation" 94-9; Knowles and Moore Companion to Conrad 82-4).

By the time of Conrad's journey to the Congo in 1890, the leading European colonial powers, Britain and France, for example, controlled about more than half of the world's territories. It was also the period of what Brantlinger calls "a militantly expansionist New Imperialism" ("Rule" 856), in which imperial governments and educated societies put forward various schemes for the civilization of the so-called primitive or savage societies. As Youngs writes, "Europe's mythologizing of Africa in general and of the Congo in particular means that fact and fiction do sometimes overlap" ("Africa/The Congo" 156). In fact the very image of the Congo had been a strongly mythical one, namely the Congo as the essence of Africa.

Thus by the time of the "discovery" of the Congo in the Post-Enlightenment European popular imagination, it had become the image par excellence of the difficult terrain, illness, and the abode of humanity in its mostly primitive state, as represented in Hegel's, influential Vorlesungen über die Philosophie der Weltgeschichte, or Lectures on the Philosophy of World History (1830). Thus when Conrad arrived in Matadi, Congo, there had already existed a massive inter-textual reference to the Congo in explorers' accounts, missionary reports, ethnographic literature, journalism, armchair travellers, and novelists such as Rider Haggard, author of King Solomon's Mines (1885). Yet again, by 1890, much of the Congo area had become the private property of Belgium's King Leopold II (beginning in 1879). In 1885, the European powers met at the Berlin Conference and sanctioned much of the Congo as the Congo Free State under the control of King Leopold II (Hochschild *Ghost* 2-10). It was also in 1890 that the Congo gripped the popular imagination of the European reading public in both the unspeakable activities and the travel accounts of Leopold's agent, Henry Morton Stanley, who published, in the same year, his sensational account of the Congo, *In Darkest Africa* (1890).

Finally, Conrad's travels in the Congo took place against the background of the pervasive belief within the European literati of the moral and intellectual superiority of western Europeans or the white race, and "the consolidation of narratives of progress, development, scientific advance, and white supremacy; those were ideologies that made imperialism possible" (Carr "Modernism" 73). And as a "white" British citizen, an agent of a powerful predatory, imperial Company, Conrad himself must have been conscious of his privileged position relative to that of the indigenous people.

The Mobile Profile

Conrad's diary consists of a central subject, a dominant body, the writing-seeing "I" moving through real and imaginative geographies, bodies and landscapes. It encodes a narrative of adventure, an adventure anchored to the body of a first-person narrator, who is also a traveller (traveller-narrator). This travelling narrator employs the situation, action, and "character" (identity) of the other in the form of a perspective on the other's body and landscape (biogeography). To be sure the diary as a whole is the invisible Body, whose invisibility allows it to plot, so to speak, its narrative representations on physiognomies and physical difference itself. Moreover, the diary format foregrounds a mobile profile of the Congo: the author, the invisible yet visible body, maintains its semantic authority (over other bodies) to the extent it is able to tell their story, to narrate their situation (pleasant, unpleasant, exotic), and their actions (moving, stationary), and so on.

The narrative of the diary consists of a number of bodies journeying through, and at the same time encountering and "negotiating" physical and bodily geographies. There is the central body (the I-body) which plots its physical and imaginative activities; the consequential body, the ailing body of Prosper Harou (a Belgian agent of the Societé); the active yet docile bodies of the carriers (about thirty-one in all). Interestingly, all the people in the diary are described in the light of the situation of their body: sick, heavy, ugly, Negroid, and so on. The narrative proceeds from a specific place (space) to a specific physiognomy (body), and vice versa, and then to "character", or what Foucault (*The Order of Things*) would call the signs lodged in their bodies (the qualities of being "good", "bad", etc.); and finally to "significance" (the implication of character, or affective states, e.g. "fine", "beautiful", "ugly"). This process may be called, following Shortland[2], a "physiognomical reading of character from the make-up and appearance of the face and body ("Skin Deep" 22).

One effect of the mobile profile is that while the author, or his body, is on the move, the diary, as a transpositional discourse, strives for "synchronic essentialism", immobility, or what Bhabha calls the "signifiers of stability" (Location 71). For example, while the diary is strongly marked by the date entry, which implies diachrony or development, the writing of the diary, on the other hand, is marked by tense and indexicality. This indicates that Conrad must have struggled with the diary, by constantly re-writing or re-working it while on the beaten track. Thus as writing, the diary is, and exists only as, a documentary account of travelling, written, for the most part, after the events it describes had already taken place, and therefore is, to this extent, a reflection, textually and rhetorically, on the events of the journey, on the past (extra-travel reflection).

Moreover, the diary conveys the disjunctive effects of a journey or travel in that it resists the immediacy of sight or visibility: it announces the central subject's configuration of the objects of visibility and those of his writing (the retrospective textual re- presentation of visual phenomena). Nevertheless, the diary is, in an important sense, a "filing system" for the author's gaze, or visual inspection of bodies and spaces.

The Gaze

The mobile profile of the native body that the diary provides is predicated on the power of the gaze, the gaze of the speaking body, the traveller-narrator. He not only inscribes the condition of the body ("the dead body", "the sick", "the good camp place") but also gazes upon the sensuous native body. Indeed the diary exists as such only because the writing body is also the gazing body, the body with visual authority, which assumes the "commanding view" in the encounter between different kinds of body, expatriate and indigenous. The gaze alone constructs, orders, and arranges the significance or otherwise of the indigenous body's visual economy[3]. As a text, as a system of writing, the diary is the *differential framework* for the gaze of the author; for by "spacing out", so to speak, bodies and spaces, the diary is intimately related to the gaze and to visualism[4], in that it conceals its dependence on the author-body, and assumes the power and gaze of the author- body by integrating, or rather blurring the distinction between, the journey and the gaze, the visual activity of the monadic subject and the documentary activity of the demiurgic hero (of the diary). This is why it is crucial to clarify the basis of the diary's demiurgic existence as the encodation of visibility.

In entry after entry, Conrad is the writing and gazing body; he takes the commanding view, the panoramic vista, the panoptical view, or what Pratt calls "the Monarch-of-all-I-Survey" view (*Imperial Eyes* 202). It is from this vantage point that the writing body even attains a consciousness of its situation (whether sick, exhausted, or pleased), that of the landscape (whether smelly or clouded or calm), and that of the other-body (whether the porters are lazy, Harou is sick, or the albino-face is "horrid chalky white with pink blotches" 165).

The author-diarist is able to encode the body of the native as a semantically producible matrix, as the subject of articulation, only because he is also the visual subject: for it is in the visual apprehension of the native body that the entire Congo becomes a visual scene, a scene which is then "reconstructed" as the textual signified, that is, invested with a meaning (the body-as-text). Here, the author-diarist-seer moves, as has been mentioned, from the visible nature of the body to its visual significance, that is, the author is the seeing-body which, in beholding the native body, also discloses its sign (virtues or otherwise). This visual manifold is what Duncan calls "double erasure and inscription" ("Dis-Orientation" 156). From this perspective, the diary is the "container", so to speak, of the story of the author's visual activity, for it connects visualism with the whole semantic network that connects the author's sight with his signification (meaning- production) of the objects of sight or visibility. It is here, in the diary, that the visual and the textual, the verbal and the visible come together. In this sense, the author's body, unlike the gazed body of the native, becomes a subject in its own right, and capable of ocular self-expression, or what Bourdieu calls "objectivism", a process whereby visual imaging is translated into relatively enduring textual traces.

Objectivism constitutes the social world as a spectacle presented to an observer who takes up a 'point of view' on the action, who stands back so as to observe it and, transferring into his object the principles of his relation to the object, conceives of it as a totality for cognition alone, in which all interactions are reduced to symbolic exchanges. (*Distinction* 96)

This may be illustrated by the manner in which the writing body "spreads on" the native body specific attributes of significance; the way in which the gaze becomes an active excavation of the body, and the meaning (meaningfulness) of the body:

> *Friday, 4th July.* Left Camp at 6 a.m. after a very unpleasant night... saw another dead body lying by the path in an attitude of meditative repose. In the evening three women, of whom one albino passed our camp; horrid chalky white with pink blotches; red eyes; red hair; features very negroid and ugly. (165)

This is how Conrad "disciplines" the gazed body: here the gaze, the dominant body's gaze, highlights the surface of the other body as difference; its appeal to the surface of the other body is a strategic move in that it conveys a semantic (descriptive) mastery over the latter (the strange and bizarre, the ugly body, the grotesque physiognomy).

Notice that the author-body is capable of normative judgement of the native body to the extent that it is the controlling body- consciousness: it is at the centre of the surrounding bodies, yet apart from them, so that the better it organizes and classifies them according to a hierarchy of values or criteria (its own system of value). Thus Conrad's power of description in the diary is based on his existence in his own diary as the observer-body, and the other bodies as his observed, or perceptual field. Conrad's interpretation of the native body as "ugly" reflects the "circumspective force" of his gaze, which, at the same time, suppresses the "answering gaze" of the native body. Thus in this "disproportionate economy of sight the writer preserves, on a material and human level, the relations of power inherent in the larger system of order" (Spurr 17).

This larger system of order is "difference", or the differential network which marks off or demarcates asymmetries and significations. For example, in the entry for "Thursday, 3rd July", the inscribing body-consciousness notes that the landscape of the Congo has mostly dense vegetation, so dense that the "villages [are] quite invisible" (164). This observation about the "invisibility" of the villages registers the dialectic of difference in the diary: the visual economy of the gazing body is dependent on the discriminating documentary powers of the representation of the visual as a desire for presence. The presence of the absence of the native body is therefore rendered as an opposition (invisibility); but which, if the diary is to cohere as a literary symbol of visuality (the gazed physiognomical specimens), must be re-inscribed as the absence (invisibility) of a presence (meaning; significance).

Difference

That is why, in the diary, the gaze is the gaze of difference, and, as we have seen above, of pathology, the death, as it were, of the living reality (of the Congo). (See, on this, Gilman, Difference and Pathology). Just as the hills and valleys are distant and difficult to explore; just as the forest is dark and dense, the sky cloudy, and the water muddy, so the native body is exotic and utterly "deficient" in that it is always "suffering", "sickly", "horrid", and "negroid" (165). In other words, the native body is the body of difference like the "dead body of a Backongo. Shot? Horrid smell." (163). In the diary the native body is used to codify and fix difference; for not only is it an extension of the landscape but also, like the landscape, accessible only as an image of the landscape. That is, the writing body inscribes the landscape and the native body all at once: the Congo nature is the body of the native; it is its "great body without organs"[5]. Conversely, the native body is the body-organ of the Congo: neither the Congo landscape nor the native body has or possesses a "full body". Indeed in the diary, as in Heart of Darkness, neither the landscape nor the native body has "subjectivity" in the form of "voice-consciousness". Thus the aesthetic ontology of ugliness and discomfort, which the diary encodes, applies in equal measure to both the native space and body:

> Harou not very well. Mosquitos-fogs-beastly! Glad to see the end of this stupid tramp. Feel rather seedy. Sun rose red. Very hot day. (171)

Notice, in the passage above, the endemic pathology of even the natural world, for the Congo is "red in tooth and claw": it makes Harou, the white man, sick; it breeds the large quantities of mosquitoes which are the menacing yet constant presence in the Congo; and harbours the "red" sun, the fiery heat of the land.

Another framing device of difference in the diary is the representation of the indigenous body as a pathological specimen, as seen in scenes of a dead or dying native body The diary catalogues scenes of dead native bodies all smelling horridly; or the absent presence of the native body in the form of a skeleton which is "tied up to a post" (169), in contrast to the "white body" (white man's body) which lies in a grave or under a "heap of stones"[6].

In the diary, only the native-black body dies and decomposes, and is left to the mercy of the elements. It is as if the native body is allowed to "return", as it were, to the native landscape, or rather as if the diary is intent on registering the essential symmetry of native space and native body in the form of their ultimate, cosmic reconciliation. Notice that the expatriate body, in the form of the dead body of the white man, lies hidden, so to speak, from the elements: it is "housed", secured, in a grave, under a "heap of stones in the form of a cross" (169). While the native body rots and disintegrates in the open landscape, without a sign of culture or religion (the cross), the "non-nature" body is the sign of culture and civilization ("the grave"; "the cross"). In essence, then, while the native body dies, the non-native body lives as an icon of a larger, cosmic event or sign (civilization). It is this, therefore, which marks the distinction between the two bodies. As Spurr writes, for most western writers, ... the body is that which is most proper to the primitive, the sign by which the primitive is represented. The body, rather than speech, law, or history, is the essential defining characteristic of primitive peoples. (*Rhetoric* 22)

This does explain why the natives in the diary live and die in their bodies and in their natural landscape while the non-native white bodies live and die in a civilizational body politic, or the sign of civilization (the grave; the cross; a heap of stones, etc). In the differential economy of pathology, the native body is also a bodyscape which, like the landscape, allows the observer-narrator- writer to set up what may be called a semiosis of exoticism in which the body is the archetypal site of difference itself. The "negroid" body is described as "ugly"; the albino body, with its red eyes, red hair and blotches signifies the unpleasantness (to the observer) of the different. The observer encounters three women, whose names he does not mention, but only their skin colour, eyes, hair, and nostrils, in short their physiognomy. It is this physiognomy that is dismissed as "ugly". The women are displaced into their body organs; they exist only to signify the anasthetic by which the observer defines, catalogues, and classifies the native body. As specimens, the women-bodies lack, by implication, "grace" and "symmetry" because the physicality of their presence is almost horrifyingly surreal. The parts and surfaces of their bodies are highlighted as a sign of essential difference; the women-bodies are, to this extent, speechless, anesthetized, and objectified as an index of an anti-aesthetic (ugliness). In fact the seeing-body uses their bodies as a convenient mechanism by which he effects the translation of the visual and the verbal.

As Low suggests, the "appeal to surfaces is strategic to a discourse of racism" ("His Stories?" 108). Note, for example, how Conrad "spreads on" the black women the fetish of race and skin colour. Note also the manner by which the author reduces the women to a specific part or surface of the body, namely the face. In the diary, the albino-body in particular is an anti-aesthetic or antiart, that is, almost "white" but not quite. That is, as content, the black body lacks a form (a signifying form, a beautiful form). In this way, the diary seeks to exhibit the native body by displaying it as the mark (symbol) of difference (which is also another form of "expulsion" from the norm). (See, on this, Hall, "The Spectacle of the Other" 259).

As Lidchi would argue, such a display is also a displacement since it creates, and it is itself a creation of, a representation of the other as an artifact (Lidchi, "Poetics" 153). To this extent, then, the albino-woman- body-physiognomy has been "fetishized" into a phantasmal body, or rather is reduced to a grotesque body-part, whose sensory existence (sensuous wealth) is reduced to nothing. Thus in the diary there are no whole native humans, only the "severed parts of the black body" (Lidchi 107).

Yet there are situations in which the native body is useful to the observer-writer, as when the body labours for him, carries him in a hammock, and transports his goods. In these contexts, the black body is not a sensuous body (with a sensuous plenitude) but a labouring body, whose defining physical characteristic is muscle power.

The Muscular Body

In pro-slavery literature, from Edward Long's *History of Jamaica* (1774) to Hegel's *Lectures on the Philosophy of World History* (1830), the black body has been described under the sign of labour or work (labour supply). In the diary, the only value of the native body is a material one as a porter or carrier (of the white man's body and goods): Conrad's body is carried by a large number of bodies. The black body's function is as a labour supply. In this sense, the black body has a utilitarian rather than an aesthetic value. This indeed is the black body's "burden". The diary records the central body's feuds with the labouring bodies. The other white body, Harou, is constantly sick; is on many occasions unable to walk, and therefore has to be carried, even though he/it is large and heavy, and weighs about 120 kilogrammes, weight which the carrier-bodies find very oppressive (169-70).

The diary records one "row with carriers" after another, their great difficulty in carrying the rather bulky Harou, and their petty quarrels and "blows with sticks" (171). Not once does Conrad describe any of the porters: their individuality is suppressed. While the white bodies are individuals with specific social markers of name and address, and whose proper names are mentioned, for example, Roger Casement, GFW Hope, Captain Purdy, Prosper Harou, Mr. Louette, the natives are only bodies and physiognomies, without proper names, social markers, or address. Here, the black body or form is "isolated" and invested with a larger-than-life significance. Because the diarist's expected "long march to get to Nsona" (165) would be impossible without the carriers, the black body of the carrier assumes, for this reason, great significance for the diarist-narrator. For without the labouring native body, the narrator would have died: when sick he is nourished by the native body; he is carried around in a hammock by the labouring body, which also acts as his informant, cook, guide, bodyguard, helper, and nurse. Yet in the diary such a "body" is still treated as a mere "spectacle", and a cipher. This is what Mercer has called "the isolation effect" whereby the indigenous body is invested with the attributes of a beast of burden, fit only for labour. ("Imaging" 145).

In the same manner, the image of the native body is used as a framing device in favour of the author-body: while the former is incapable of the scientific discourse of science and navigation (which further frames the diary, with its show of technical knowledge, maps, and the technology of writing), the latter is the writing-scientific subject par excellence. The diary, it should be emphasized, is full of scientific, geographic, and technical diction, the very discourse that "fixes" the reality of the speaking body and establishes the non-presence of the native body. And it is this relational representation of different kinds of bodies which serves as the semiosis by which the diary sets up, reinforces, and fortifies difference. Furthermore, it is this visible-lisible-scriptible economy of difference which gives the diary its raison d'etre and narrative (or non-narrative) power. This is because everything within the native body-space falls within the visual field of the observer-narrator; nothing in the native space escapes this visual field. Thus he is the centre of the diary whether as a discourse or as an episodic representation of events. Everything, that is, including the material presence of space, exists for the semantic consumption of the first person singular pronoun the "I"-body.

It is in that sense that the non-labouring body, the parasitical body, or rather the phenomenological-voice consciousness that is the writing subject, displaces the labouring body and assumes the position of the ontological-primary body, or what Bhabha would call the "undifferentiated whole white body" (Location 92). That is, the reader of the diary rather encounters, or is forced to encounter, as far as the representation of the native body is concerned, only a grotesque body, rather than a whole human being, despite his labouring burdens, in opposition to the formidable presence of the speaking-writing-observing subject, the bearer of singular existential propositions the demiurgic subject of travel and narration.

The Menacing Body

70

Taken as a whole, Conrad's diary is a gloomy characterization of the Congo both as a landscape and as a bodily economy. The diary notes that most days are "gloomy" and the wind is "remarkably cold" (168). Almost everyone, except some of the natives, namely the carriers, is in poor health. There is a constant reference to the mosquitoes, and to mosquito-infested swamps. The ascent up the mountain or hill is "long"; everything is a constant "bother" (162). At night, there are wild, threatening cries or "shouts and drumming" in the villages (164-65). Indeed there are hardly any "good camping places". Everywhere, "water is scarce and bad" (163). The trees are unusually "tall and thick" (164). They show no compassion: they seem as if they would "grow through" the body of the observer. The sun is "heavy" (166) and "very hot" (167); in many instances, there is "no shade" (166); and things are "wretched" (166), so that, on the whole, "the country presents a confused wilderness of hills, landslips on their sides showing red" (167). As for the "hammock carriers", they are a treacherous and feuding lot. On one occasion, they even threaten to "go on strike", that is, refuse to enter service or carry the large but sick Harou (169-70).

The wider point is that the Congo is a source of anxiety for Conrad; it is also a threat to the narrator's hegemonic discourse of visual-verbal representation because it seems to defy an unproblematic representation within the observer's visual and semantic economy; and because the "strong white man" is always sick, and dependent on a mass of native bodies for his survival in an alien environment. Hence, his descriptive manifold is always at the verge of breaking down. However, it reasserts itself in the form of Conrad's pained self-assertion and textual anguish, which routinely show up in the elliptical and terse literary style of the diary.

All through the diary, the observer-narrator struggles to re-assert himself, or rather his special powers of visual comprehension and textual nomination of the real, in the face of the oppressive ontological presence of the landscape. In many parts of the diary, there is an unstated connection between the body economy of the narrator and the natural economy of the landscape; and between sensibility (the ability of the author to "feel") and the natural economy. In fact, in a sense, the diary is the cogito's uneasy "victory" over the inert, chaotic natural and bodily landscapes. This is the case because the only instances in which the narrator "feels good" and, therefore, returns to normality and good health ("comfortable and pleasant halt" 167) is when he meets fellow Europeans such as Messrs Heyn and Jaeger, Mr. Roger Casement, Mr. Underwood, and Mrs. Comber:

> *Tuesday, 8th July.* Left at 9 A.M. About ten minutes from camp left main Govt [Government] path for the Manyanga track. Sky overcast. Rode up and down all the time, passing a couple of villages. The country presents a confused wilderness of hills, landslips on their sides showing red... Arrived at Manyanga at 9 A.M. Received most kindly by Messrs. Heyn and Jaeger. Most comfortable and pleasant halt. (166-67)

> Sunday, 27th. Left at 8 A.M. Sent luggage carriers straight to Luasi, and went themselves around by the Mission of Sutili. Hospitable reception by Mrs. Comber. All the missio. [missionaries] absent. The looks of the whole establishment eminently civilized and very refreshing to see after the lots of tumbled down hovels in which the State & Company agents are content to live. Fine buildings. Position on a hill. Rather breezy. (167)

Now it is clear that this "civilized and very refreshing" station is the only one of its kind in the overwhelmingly gloomy environment. Not even the carriers on whom the white man's survival depends can match Mrs. Comber's "hospitable reception" of the narrator. Here, there are no mosquitoes, brackish water, sickness, or "a long and painful climb up a very steep hill" (170). In those passages, then, the narrator attempts to demarcate the two supposedly different space-bodies on the basis of their normative appeal or otherwise to his sensibility. It is here, also, that the narrator foregrounds his bodily economy: the native space-body is *natural* (savage and primitive), while the European space-body is *cultural* (as a mark or marker of civilization, European civilization, which is, in the last analysis, normative). The former is *lexical* (merely talked about as a negative presence); the latter is a sublime presence (inspiring, comfortable, delightful, and life-enhancing).

In this way, the threatening native body-space is allegorized, and turned from a source of anxiety and interdiction to a metaphorical- rhetorical image of an unruly yet conquered sign, the very familiar end of an opposition with the civilized (anti-culture). This is the only way by which the narrator can impose order (form) on the unruly native body-space (content). By thus writing up the other, he makes it less threatening since the other is now, in the diary, visible, lisible, and legible (rendered familiar and "normative" within the discourse of difference).

It is in this sense that Conrad's diary is a fictional representation of the native body, for in it the native body has vanished: it has become a palimpsest, written over, and turned into a superscription in that the diary's sustained description of the negative features of the native space-body is, and has been, a preparation both for the narrative ego's evaluation of it as a difference and an other (of the same and familiar) and for its chiastic contrast with the normative the signifier for

73

European civilization. In this sense, then, the diary as a whole is a reinvention of the native body as the phantasmal body, the substitute body, that formidable body of difference whose presence, Shortland suggests, must be erased by racist and colonialist narrative:

> The colonizer of the body surface lays down the rules, formulates the law of reading, and sets into play pretence autonomy of signifiers. Text and image put into circulation body, face, writing, but only the last possesses any freedom of development. ("Skin Deep" 45)

Fluid Interchanges

The preceding arguments may be objected to on the ground that the diary is a non-fictional mechanism which allows a faithful recording of reality. Indeed the diary, especially one strongly marked by temporal facts, namely dates, geography, proper names, and actual, historical events, has a ring of strong empirical realism about it. In fact, as we have noted above, many a Conrad scholar (for example, Knowles and Moore) has used the diary as a window on Conrad's own life-experiences, his *leben welt*, and as a source of his early fiction on the assumption that non-fictional texts, such as the diary, represent the world as it really is[7].

Our argument is that the diary, as writing, is a representational device, and a fictional one as that first because, as Derrida argues, writing, as substitute signification, "never touches the soil, as it were" (in the diary a list of facts is transformed into a narrative, or rather narrativized, i.e. the events or facts "speaking themselves" as a story or fiction); and second because insofar as the authorial "I" of the diary has to see before he recognizes, that is, sees before he says, the diary (the record of visibly screened objects) is the consummate, or consummation of, the perceived, longed-for unity, of form (visibility) and content (writing, text), symbol (body) and meaning (normativity).

In the diary, Conrad attempts to bridge the gap, as it were, between seeing and saying, visibility and description, words and objects. Conrad could thus not rely on a mere nomination of the visible alone (otherwise we would have no historical record of his travels in the Congo). He must thus have recourse to textuality, to writing as the supplement (and supplementation) to visibility. The diary, as a form of textuality, brings together (unsuccessfully at any rate) the objects of visibility, the screened objects of visual apprehension, and the language in which the objects are described, re-presented, or narrated. To this extent, the diary is truly a vehicle for the re-tracing of visible objects so that they become legible, and, to use a Derridean metaphor, the repetition of the same.

Nevertheless, Conrad must pay a heavy price for this, from an empirical realist point of view. That is, Conrad must cease to be a flesh-and-blood person; must thus be a fictional subject if he is to remain the subject of writing. This is because the enterprise of the diary (or diary-writing) requires, and is itself, a representation; for a purely visual apprehension of the native body or space must also consist in a resistance to representation (metaphorization). For example: Conrad would have us believe in the diary that he was/is in touch with the real, intransitive Congo space-body; that, in other words, his "entries" were/are true, immediate, and matter-of-fact. This, however, is not possible: to remain the subject of assertions, the authorial consciousness of the diary, Conrad must also re-present himself as, at least, a corporal image in the diary. That is, he, as real author, has inevitably to refer to himself as a "written self" within the diary. This means that he also, unwittingly, alludes to a fictional Conrad within the diary. Here then, we have three Conrads: investing eye (the traveling, mobile and active Conrad; the seeing-man); a writing subject (Conrad the real author); and the written subject of proposition (the textual trace, the narratee Conrad).

This is possible only in a fictional situation. Yet this is what the presence of the diary implies, namely that the real author (of the diary) must, to transform the visual image of the native body-space into the signified content of (his) experience (the diary content) and at the same time, aspire to a fictional, metaphorical, and metonymic presence within the very symbolic resources of textuality (the diary format or frame narrative) that he deploys.

Thus the diary, or the writing of it, makes possible a situation in which a single body becomes more than one body; in which the writing self (body) writes itself into the form of its activity (the diary), and, simultaneously, preserves, presents, and re-presents its activity (including the writing of the diary) as both the outcome of the journey (of seeing or visual exploration) and the activity of the journey (inscription) as meaning and as text. In this sense, then, the diary affords Conrad a situation (of writing) in which he not only sets up the act of seeing but also the representation of the seeing. Thus the inscription, his inscription, of the native body implies, hides, and re-integrates, the representation of the visual explorer, the body which now re-inscribes, and, in effect, writes over, the other the native body and space. As Derrida would argue, writing is the sensible and the finite, and on the side of "artifice" (*Grammatology* 15).

The implication of this is that Conrad's *The Congo Diary* is a representation (idea) of representation (image) because all the objects which the diary names or re-traces, namely the concrete realism of bodies, spaces, landscapes, rivers,

76

trees, markets, people, boxes, carriers, hammocks, the Congo hills and valleys, all these are nothing but writing, nothing but the differential productiveness of inscription and metaphor. This is why beyond and behind *The Congo Diary* there is nothing but writing, that is, "supplements substitute significations which could only come forth in a chain of differential traces" (159). This is the import of Pfeiffer's insight that where there is only body-space or mere voice-consciousness, there is only the "simultaneity of the absent and the fabricated" ("Black Hole" 200). Yet, it is an absence and a fabrication with concrete ideological and philosophic, even practical consequences:

> "...the nomination of the visible is no idle metaphysic, no disinterested revealing of the world's wonders. It is, on the contrary, a mode of thinking and writing wherein the world is radically transformed into an object of possession. The gaze is never innocent or pure, never free of mediation by motives which may be judged noble or otherwise. The writer's eye is always in some sense colonizing the landscape, mastering and portioning, fixing zones and poles, arranging and deepening the scene as the object of desire. (Spurr 27)

Conclusion

We have underlined the potent mixture of the literary propaedeutics of travel (or the mobile profile), the fictionalizing phenomenology of visualism, and the semiosis of textuality in Conrad's representation of non-European biogeography, spaces, and bodies. We have seen that the diary, with its lack of pretence for the autonomy of signifiers, its commitment to textual materiality and ontological realist representation is, paradoxically, one of the most convenient and powerful structures of representation.

Conrad's diary-writing, and *The Congo Diary* itself, confirm Barthes' notion of the text as a movement of discourse which is "experienced only in an activity of production" ("From Work" 117). For *The Congo Diary* is most experienced in its production of a host of mobile structures of signs, namely the visual symbolization and textual displacement of native normativity. It is in this sense that Conrad's diary is a textuality, a semiotic field (rather than a mimetic one), and a tissue of repetitions, appellations, demarcations (difference) and practices (of rhetorical networks of incorporation, colonization, and debasement). It is equally in this sense that Conrad's diary is both an index of what Said calls "the worldliness of the text" (*The World* 31) and of Derrida's concept of "violence of the letter", or the "anthropological war" (*Grammatology* 107).

That is, Conrad's diary is worldly, since it names an ontological presence (the Congo), and other proper names. To this extent, it is a cultural and historical production, with a definite, identifiable origin or source, all of which may be traced to the history and legacy of colonialism and imperialism. On the other hand, however, the diary is also a representation in which the author, or the central subject, employs native spaces and bodies within the linguistic and symbolic shape and structures of a vampiric consciousness and self-generated intelligibility, and figurative mastery in which the native or non-European space and body disintegrate under the racist-colonialist gaze, and "displaced into signs of bestiality, genitalia, and grotesquerie" (*Location* 92).

The diary's substitution of a surface of the body (skin colour and organ) for the whole human subject (a person, a bio-geographical identity) is the effect, rather than the cause, of a representational production or practice in which the spatial freedom (bio- geographic exploration) inaugurated by

78

capitalist modernity (imperialism), the visual economy of the gaze, and the infinite deferment of textuality (différance)[8] are deployed against the non- European or indigenous spaces, bodies, and cultures all in an effort to fix and secure their utter difference from the Same (Europe) in the interest of imperial representation.

Chapter Four

Apport de l'œuvre de Jacques Roumain

C. J. Okolo

HAÏTIEN, né en 1907 à Port-au-Prince Jacques Roumain a laissé des œuvres importantes, au total onze ouvrages dans plusieurs genres: nouvelles, romans, récits, essais, poèmes. Nous nous intéressons à quatre de ces ouvrages: Poèmes " Le Nouveau Sermon Nègre" La Montagne Ensorcelée, La Proie et L'Ombre, et Gouverneurs de La Rosée. Notre choix de ces quatre ouvrages s'explique par le fait qu'ils contiennent le message maître de Roumain qui, surtout, a prêché une nouvelle prise de conscience du Noir. Egonu (1982) constate qu'aujourd'hui, les critiques littéraires et sociologues mettent de plus l'accent sur l'étude du conditionment sociologiques des œuvres littéraires et qu'on commence aussi à reconnaître l'importance de l'influence que peuvent exercer les œuvres sur les faits sociaux.1 Lilyan Kesteloot cité par Egonu (1982) remarque que les œuvres nées au sien d'un ensemble des faits sociaux qu'elles reflètent "réagissent à leur tour sur la réalité, exerçant sur elle une pression et peuvent accélérer la maturation des crises sociales et politiques."2

'Le livre' dit Dago Lezou (1972) "fait de l'écrivain un stratège et un éveilleur de conscience, un guide".3 Aujourd'hui chaque pays d'Afrique selon sa position géographique, sa constitution ethnique et sa situation économique a ses problèmes particuliers. Ces problèmes semblent avoir un poids insurmontable, ce qui fait que la masse de peuple croupisse dans la misère, et la pauvreté. Peut-elle jamais en sortir? C'est là la genèse de ce travail. Selon Michel Zeraffa (1971) "La sociabilité du roman devait lui confier une place et des fonctions culturelles, politiques, idéologiques considérables".4 La création littéraire est non seulement un reflet de la société mais aussi un instrument puissant et une force visant à la transformation sociale. Une question se pose : Quel est l'apport de la transformation sociale dans l'œuvre de Jacques Roumain aux pays d'Afrique y compris la diaspora? Ce travail cherche à répondre à cette question. Ce faisant nous allons d'abord examiner la société haïtienne de l'époque de Jacques Roumain. Ceci nous permettra de comparer la réalité historique et la réalité romanesque et de voir l'apport de la transformation sociale dans les œuvres de notre choix.

Haïti la première république noire de notre époque est un pays marqué par beaucoup de révoltes notamment celle de 1804 qui a donné naissance au pays. Les Noirs constituent la plus grand partie de la population suivis par les mulâtres. De 1915 à1934, Haïti a été occupé par les Américains qui avaient blessé la fierté des Haïtiens par leur attitude dépourvue de tact. Le pouvoir était aux mains des bourgeois mulâtres qui collaboraient avec les occupants. Ils vivaient dans la seule poursuite de leurs intérêts personnels, alors que la masse haïtienne croupissait dans la misère. La pauvreté du pays était encombrante, le pays était dévasté, l'égoïsme et l'improbité régnaient. Entre 95% et 98% de la population était illettrée, l'ignorance régnait suprême. Bien que la fertilité du sol eut été la ressource principale d'Haïti, l'agriculture et la vie paysanne étaient restées au niveau primitif. Le démarrage de l'agriculture dépendait de la restauration de l'irrigation, mais on manquait le capital et l'habileté directionnel nécessaires.

Il n'y avait pas d'intérêt dans la protection des forêts. Quelques mornes étaient très boisés les autres étaient dénudes. La santé publique était dans une condition déplorable5 Il y avait l'émigration : certains sont partis pour Cuba pour travailler aux plantations de cane à sucre. Ils y gagnaient mieux qu'en Haïti. Un grand nombre d'entre eux est d'ailleurs rentré après l'occupation. Ces conditions avaient améliorées vers la fin de l'occupation. La santé publique s'était améliorée mais la condition des paysans n'avait pas changé.

Cette situation .regrettable d'Haïti est le sujet des œuvres de Jacques Roumain que nous avons choisies. Dans les deux romans, Gouverneurs de la Rosée et La Montagne Ensorcelée et dans les nouvelles de La Proie et L'Ombre, se trouvent reconstitués deux mondes où a évolué l'adolescent Roumain. D'un côté (La Proie et L'Ombre) le monde des mulâtres riches et des intellectuels petit bourgeois sans vrai projet social d'un autre côté (Gouverneurs de la Rosée et La Montagne Ensorcelée) les villages de montagnes où des paysans sans lumière vivaient, prisonniers de leur routine, accablées de la pauvreté, de la misère et de l'angoisse.6

La transformation sociale consiste en un effort pour modifier une situation donnée dans un sens favorable, à modifier une situation de déséquilibre pour établir un équilibre. Une lecture attentive de l'œuvre (poèmes, récits, nouvelles, roman) de Jacques Romain nous révèle que la réalité romanesque reflète ce déséquilibre, un déséquilibre à l'image de la réalité sociale haïtienne. Dans les ouvrages le romancier entreprend la transformation de cette société. Le poème "Nouveau sermon nègre" fait un appel aux nègres de se ressaisir et se révolter contre les forces oppressantes.

Nous ne prierons plus

Notre révolte s'élève comme le cri de l'oiseau de tempête au-dessus
du clapotement pourri des marécages
Nous ne chanterons plus les tristes spirituals désespérés
Un autre chant jaillit de nos gorges Nous déployons nos rouges
drapeaux Tachés du sang de nos justes
Sous ce signe nous marcherons Sous ce signe nous marcherons
Debout les damnés de la terre
Debout les forçats de la faim[7]

La prise de conscience et la révolte qu'il démontre
dans "Nouveau sermon nègre" est un départ de la
contemplation et la résignation vues dans les poèmes
"Insomnie", "Noir" et "Calme".[8] La prise de conscience
évoquée dans "Nouveau sermon nègre" se voit d'avantage
dans le poème "Sales nègres". Là il s'agit d'un refus. Roumain
affirme que les nègres n'acceptent plus d'être des sales nègres.

que les nègres n'acceptent plus ... d'être vos niggers vos sales
nègres ...
car nous aurons choisi notre jour le jour des sales nègres
des sales indiens des sales hindous
des sales indochinois des sales arabes
des sales malais des sales juifs
des sales prolétaires
Et nous voici debout

Tous les damnés de la terre tous les Justiciers
Marchant à l'assaut de vos casernes et de vos banques
comme une forêt de torches funèbres pour en finir
une fois pour
toutes avec ce monde de nègres
de niggers
de sales nègres[9]

La Montagne ensorcelée Un récit paysan nous présente
une société accablée par la misère. "Le village est pauvre, la

terre crayeuse se craquelle comme l'écorce, la récolte ne vaut rien". "La nuit qui passe cède au jour lui abandonnant sa mélancolie lasse", Le jour n'est que "la certitude de longues heures pénibles d'une lutte âpre dans la chaleur torride avec la glèbe rebelle".10 Il y a aussi le fléau qui attaque les enfants et les bêtes. Après la sécheresse la pluie tombe toute la journée et la récolte est gâtée. L'angoisse pèse sur le village.

Conscients de leur malheur les villageois se réunissent pour chercher des solutions. Mais c'est un monde ignorant. Cette ignorance est liée aux pratiques traditionnelles du village. Or "la conscience collective dans une communauté traditionnelle a tendance à recourir facilement à une métaphysique absolue chaque fois qu'elle est confrontée à un phénomène nouveau, inattendu, non conventionnel".11 Pour les villageois c'est la sorcellerie qui apporte cette misère, donc la solution réside dans le meurtre d'une vieille femme et de sa fille (Les prétendues sorcières.)

Ici Jacques Roumain nous montre que la transformation sociale ne se réalise pas dans l'ignorance. Le meurtre n 'est qu'une action brutale et inhumaine née de l'incapacité de comprendre que la sécheresse est un phénomène naturel résultant probablement du déboisement du paysage.

La première nouvelle de La Proie et l'Ombre "Préface à la vie d'un bureaucrate", dépeint une société corrompue, hypocrite, bassement bourgeoise qui brise les intellectuels mais que les mulâtres haïtiens synthétisent parfaitement. Pour les mulâtres tout va bien, mais Michel, l'intellectuel, se sent déchiré de l'intérieur. La joie l'envahissait, au moment de son retour de l'Europe, mais cinq ans plus tard il se trouve toujours incapable de s'adapter à la société Porte au princienne. La vie n'a plus de sens pour lui, car résume-t-il, "J'ai étreint la vie trop fort, trop bien. Je l'ai saisi à la gorge, étouffée"12

Son incapacité de trouver une solution à ce conflit fait naître en lui de la haine pour sa belle-mère mulâtre qui au contraire synthétise parfaitement cette société. Ce n'est que cette haine qui lui rend la vie supportable. "il s'y agrippe comme un noyé à une racine"13

Il a essayé de prêcher l'indigénisme à l'élite haïtienne mais cela ne leur vaudra rien. A la maison 'sa prison' il reste étranger à ses enfants et ne cesse de rendre sa femme malheureuse. Il se voit comme un raté aux dents agacées par la vie. Son passé l' accentue parce qu'il a échoué dans la politique. Il écrit des manifestes, des poèmes et un roman là encore c'est l'échec car personne ne les lit.

En outre Il se débarrassera de cette vie d'amertume aussitôt qu'il acceptera la place offerte grâce à sa belle-mère au ministère de l'intérieur, Il n'en veut pas. Il se croit avoir dépassé le niveau de moutons de panurge, pourtant ses rêves restent hors de portées. En fin emporté par la lâcheté, il cède à la demande de cette société qu'il hait tellement. Roumain démontre ici que la lâcheté ne peut rien dans la transformation d'une société quelle qu'elle soit.

La deuxième nouvelle "Propos sans suite" pour sa part montre les intellectuels bien conscients du problème de leur société mais ne font que l'analyser. Daniel, médecin, se sent pareil aux prostituées par la souffrance et le dégoût quotidien, par son impuissance et sa lâcheté devant la vie. Jean, avocat, son camarade lui fournit un bon conseil "il faut réagir". Pourtant ils ont tout ce qu'il faut pour réussir. En Haïti, réussir c'est "être avocat, ingénieur, médecin ou pire politicien, gagner de l'argent affin de pourvoir bien manger, avoir une auto et être membre d'un, cercle".14

Mais la conscience aiguë de Daniel le fait voir de telles satisfactions comme issues d'une inconscience animale. Le milieu le rend incapable de réussir à sa façon. En Haïti, "dès qu'un homme cherche sa voie droite hors celles des autres, hors celle de moutons de panurge, il est traité en brebis galeuse, dès qu'un front emerge au-dessus du niveau commun, il est écrasé"15

Le poète Emilo de sa part n'écrit plus, ayant toujours rencontré pour tout encouragement l'incompréhension. Jean remarque que ce qui manque à l'intelligence haïtienne c'est d'être plié à une discipline, ce qui veut dire tendre vers un but obstinément. Où trouver cette discipline? Dans la politique? Improbable, car en Haïti la patrie est la somme des intérêts particuliers qui se heurtent et se repoussent. N'est-ce pas ici, l'image des pays africains ?

Bien que ces intellectuels sachent qu'une réaction positive apportera des solutions ils se laissent aller pleins de tristesse, délaissés et inutiles. La vie reste un fardeau qui pèse sur eux et les fait courber de plus en plus en bas. Ils veulent tous transformer la société mais le milieu d'une résistance encombrant leur donne des frustrations.

Dans la troisième nouvelle "La veste" il s'agit de deux victimes de la crise de conscience. D'un part Savire, qui est rendu psychopathe par sa vie marquée de l'angoisse et la souffrance. Se sentant troué, déchire rapiécé comme sa veste accrochée au mur, il s'est pendu. De l'autre part se voit un autre intellectuel, qui est revenu après un séjour à l'étranger il quitte sa famille, il habite en pension, mais ne paye pas son loyer, il écrivait des vers et lisait un tas de bouquins. Ensuite on le trouve pendu.

Cette fois mourir c'est pour eux la seule issue possible car ils ne peuvent pas résoudre les conflits entre leurs vies et leurs rêves. La transformation sociale ne se réalise pas par la seule définition du problème. Il faut la recherche et l'adoption de la solution visée. En nous présentant ces personnages de la conscience aiguë, Roumain nous prépare le terrain pour son héros, le leader, le libérateur de l'opprimé.

Le livre Gouverneurs de la rosée, contrairement à ce que nous avons vu dans les autres ouvrages va plus loin. On y passe de la définition jusqu'à la solution des problèmes pour atteindre la transformation sociale. D'abord il y a une prise de conscience de problèmes de la société. La sécheresse, la misère, la désolation et l'hostilité. La vie pour les paysans est une pénitence. Il n'y a pas de consolation. Se croyant abandonnés par Dieu, les paysans se résignent et offrent des sacrifices pour apaiser les divinités. Ensuite Manuel arrive, plein de l'expérience de la vie pénible qu'il avait mené à Cuba, et conscient de la misère à Fonds Rouge (chez lui.) Il a eu une crise de conscience, ce qui le pousse à la recherche des solutions. Le courage ne lui manque pas. Il entreprend la lute contre l'ignorance.

Dans La montagne ensorcelée et dans La proie et l'ombre on n'a pas pu réaliser une transformation sociale à cause de l'ignorance et du manque du courage. Manuel entreprend ainsi l'éducation de son peuple. "C'est pas Dieu qui abandonne le nègre, c'est le nègre qui abandonne la terre et il reçoit sa punition: La sécheresse, la misère et la désolation."16

C'est traître la résignation, c'est du pareil au même que le découragement. Ça vous casse le bras. On attend des miracles et la providence, chapelet on main, sans rien faire. On prie pour la pluie, on prie pour la récolte, on dit les oraisons des saintes et des loa. Mais la providence c'est le propre vouloir du nègre de ne pas accepter le malheur, de dompter chaque jour la mauvaise volonté de la terre, de soumettre le caprice de l'eau à ses besoins, alors la terre l'appelle : cher maître, il n'y a d'autre providence que son travail d'habitant sérieux, d'autre miracle que le fruit de ses mains."17

Il leur dit aussi que les nègres sont pauvres, malheureux, et misérables à cause de leur ignorance.

> Nous ne savons pas encore que nous sommes une force. Une seule force tous les habitants, tous les nègres de plaines et des mornes réunis un jour quand nous aurons compris cette vérité nous nous lèverons d'un point â l'autre du pays et nous ferons l'assemblée générale des gouverneurs de la rosée.
> Le grand coumbite* des travailleurs de la terre pour défricher la misère et planter une vie nouvelle"18

La transformation sociale nécessite l'unité. Hoffmann (1973)parlant de la première révolte d'esclaves qui ait réussi (révolte en Saint Domingue devenu Haïti) a remarqué que c'est à l'unité que le succès du Project est redevable.19 Manuel le sait bien car il entreprend aussi la réconciliation de deux camps ennemis de Fonds Rouge. Il a la foi dans la capacité de l'homme. Par conséquent il ne se décourage pas devant la tâche apparemment impossible de trouver l'eau. C'est sa mission et son devoir.

"L'expérience"dit-il, "est le bâton des aveugles, et j'ai appris que ce qui compte c'est la rébellion, et la connaissance que l'homme est le boulanger de la vie"20

Enfin il trouve l'eau. Avec l'aide d'Anaïse, la nouvelle se répande. Or Anaïse sur la direction de Manuel a entrepris l'éducation de ses voisins sur l'importance de l'eau. Poursuivant le mouvement pour la réconciliation, Manuel se rend à la réunion du camp ennemi. Il leur explique ce qu'il faut faire pour amener l'eau au village. Le malveillant Gervilen le tue peu après. Christiane Conturie (1992) examinant la cause de la mort de Manuel remarque que pour un Jacques Roumain fidèle à ses engagements politiques, les forces du mal se situent d'abord dans la société 'La volonté de puissance, la cupidité des classes dominantes tendent toujours a écraser à les plus faibles'. Jacques Roumain continue-t-elle donne au geste de Gervilen 'le poids de la haine de tous ceux que le succès de Manuel gênerait.21 Stephen Alexis répondant à la question: Qui est Gervilen? dit que c'était le symbole de la dictature sur Haïti, de ces hommes ambitieux, jaloux de tous les succès des humbles, de ces hommes incapables de travail assidu pour le bien de tous.22 Avant de mourir Manuel donne son testament:

> Si tu préviens Hilarion(l'agent de police) ce sera encore une fois la même histoire de Saveur et Dorisca. La haine, la vengeance entre les habitants. L'eau sera perdue...Va trouver Larivoire. Dis-lui la volonté du sang qui a coulé : la réconciliation, la réconciliation pour que la vie recommence, pour que le jour se lève sur la rosée"23

Les habitants se réunissent en grand coumbite, ils construisent le canal et apportent l'eau â Fonds Rouge. La vie renaît et la société est transformée.

> Quelle est donc l'apport de cet étalage de la transformation sociale dans l'œuvre de Jacques Romain aux pays d'Afrique? Jean Paul Satre (1948) nous dit que "l'œuvre d'art est valeur parce qu'elle est d'abord un appel."24

J.M Dash (1978) a dit que pour le romancier haitien "The novel was to be a kind of sociological investigation of society which would eventually reveal universal truths of the human condition."25 Pour Sartre (1948) "L'écrivain parle à ses contemporains à ses compatriotes, à ses frères de races ou de classe."26 En conséquence, les œuvres de Roumain ne sont-elles pas destinées à l'Afrique et aux pays du tiers monde ? Quel pays d'Afrique de nos jours ne se ressemble pas à la société haïtienne que dépeint Roumain dans ces œuvres ?

L'Afrique aujourd'hui est marquée par la pauvreté, la misère la souffrance, l'ignorance, la maladie, la violence, la guerre l'injustice, voire tous les abus et les vices dont on peut imaginer. Nwokora (2000) dit que "L'Afrique reste le continent le plus bouleversé du monde…les Nigérians (comme les autres Africains) croient encore qu'ils sont 'arrivés' dès qu'ils puissent acheter une villa à Londres ou à Paris et vivre comme les blancs."[27] La masse du peuple africain comme leurs compères dans les œuvres de Jacques Roumain sont accablés par la misère, elle mène une vie pénible, une vie la même qu'une mort lente. Les leaders et les politiciens dans les pays d'Afrique à leur tour mènent une vie dépourvue de conscience sociale. Ils sont corrompus et hypocrites, Ils marginalisent et brisent la masse du peuple.

Une transformation sociale est donc exigée devant cette condition regrettable où se trouve la masse du peuple dans les pays d'Afrique. Il nous faut une prise de conscience des problèmes socio-politiques Africains comme l'a prêché Jacques Roumain dans ces ouvrages. Cette prise de conscience serait suivie d'une crise de conscience. Mais Roumain montre que les deux ne peuvent rien sans une réaction positive. Roumain est d'accord avec Malraux (1946) qui fait dit Tchen "je n'aime pas de l'humanité faite de la contemplation de la souffrance."[28] Donc en plus de la prise et la crise de conscience il nous faut le courage, l'éducation de la masse du peuple, un solide confiance dans la nature humaine et le progrès dont elle est capable, l'unité, la solidarité, la collectivité d'action, une réforme de la morale du peuple et une réforme économique par la moyenne de l'agriculture.

L'unité parmi les citoyens même parmi les pays est indisponible à la transformation sociale en Afrique. Nnolim (1992) affirme que le manque de l'unité parmi les Africains résulte dans la tragédie de Le

Monde s'Effondre de Chinua Achebe. Par contre continuet-il, Sembene Ousmane dans Les bouts de bois de Dieu démontre le résultat heureux vu quand la masse de travailleurs opprimés africains hommes, femmes, enfants, pleins de la prise de conscience, avec la solidarité, la volonté collective, la foi dans la capacité de l'homme remportent une victoire épique.29

La masse du peuple africain doit se réveiller de l'inaction et du sommeil dû à la lâcheté. La contemplation de la souffrance, la misère et l'angoisse dans lesquelles nous (la masse du peuple) nous noyons ne servent à rien. La solution des problèmes socio- économiques des pays africains ne réside non plus dans l'émigration vers L'Europe ou vers Les Etats Unis bien qu'on puisse y gagner mieux la vie comme le faisaient les Haïtiens à Cuba. Mais le future de ces émigres n'est pas du tout assurer car en vieillissant ils deviennent de moins en moins incapables de faire les travaux serviles que font la plupart d'entre eux. II faut que nous nous levions et lutter contre toutes forces oppressantes et répressives qui fait de notre vie une mort lente. Apprenons du villageois de Fonds Rouge.

Selon Frantz Fanon (1969) "La solidarité inter-africaine doit être une solidarité de fait, une solidarité d'action, une solidarité concrète en hommes". Pour lui "L'unité africaine est un principe à partir du quel on se propose de réaliser les Etats Unis d'Afrique"30 L'objectif de Roumain d'être l'avocat de son peuple se verrait plus tard chez les écrivains comme Richard Wright, Peter Abrahams, Sembene Ousmane e.t.c. Peut-être se sont ils inspirés de Jacques Roumain.

En un mot, à travers la présentation de la transformation sociale dans ses œuvres, Roumain a porté l'intérêt aux problèmes politiques, et socio-économiques actuelles de l'Afrique. L'étalage des démarches de la transformation sociale dans ces œuvres s'avère significatif voire indisponible aux pays du Tiers monde pour que la masse du peuple sorte de la misère et la pauvreté qui les écrasent.

ENGLISH TRANSLATION

The Literary Contributions of Jacques Roumain

HAITIAN, born in 1907 Harbor-Au-Prince, Jacques Roumain's important œuvres, is eleven works in several kinds: news, novels, narrations, tests, poems. We are interested in four of these works: Poems "The New Negro Sermon," "The Enchanted Mountain," "The Prey and The shade," and "Governors of The Dew." Our choice of these four works explains itself by the fact that they contain the main Roumanian message that preaches a reappraisal of Black conscience. Egonu (1982) notes that today, the literary critiques and sociologists put the accent besides on the survey of the sociological conditioning of the literary works and that one begins to recognise the influence that the works can exercise on social history.1

Lilyan Kesteloots, mentioned by Egonu (1982), remarked that the œuvres are born from a set of social facts which they reflect and react on the reality, exercising on her a pressure which can accelerate the social and political maturation.2 The literary arts says Dago Lezou (1972) makes of the writer a strategist and a custodian of conscience, a guide.3 Today each country of Africa according to its geographical position, its ethnic constitution and its economic situation, has its particular problems. These problems seem to have an insurmountable weight, which keeps the people stagnated in misery and poverty. Is she/it ever able to take some? There lies the significance of this work. According to Michel Zeraffa (1971)

The sociability of the novel has to confide in him a place and the cultural functions, policies, and ideologies are considerable.4 The literary creation is not only a reflection of the society but also a powerful instrument and a power aiming at the social transformation. A question is apt here: What is the contribution of Jacques' works to social transformation in countries of Africa including the Diaspora? This work looks for an answer to this question. First we must examine the Haitian society of the Jacques Roumain's time. It will permit us to compare the historic reality and the romantic reality and to see the contribution of the social transformation in the works of our choice.

Haiti, the first black republic of our time, is a country marked by many revolts, but especially the one of 1804 that gave birth to the country. The Blacks constitute the biggest part of the population followed by the mulattos. Since 1915 through 1934, Haiti had been occupied by the Americans who wounded the pride of the Haitians by an attitude destitute of tact. The power was in the hands of the mulatto bourgeois that collaborated with the occupants. They lived in the only pursuit of their personal interests, whereas the Haitian masses stagnated in misery. The poverty of the country was cumbersome. The country was ravaged. Selfishness and the lack of probity reigned. Between 95% and 98% of the population were illiterate and ignorance reigned supreme. Although the fertility of soil had been the main resource of Haiti agriculture and life farming had remained at the primitive level. The success of agriculture depended on the restoration of irrigation, but one missed the capital and the necessary managerial expertise. There was no law for the protection of the forests. Most lands were afforested and others very quite denuded. The public health was in a deplorable condition.5 There was mass emigration:

some left for Cuba to work in the plantations. They fared better than in Haiti. A good number of them went back after the occupation. Conditions had improved toward the end of the occupation. The public health has improved but the condition of the peasants has not changed.

This regrettable situation of Haiti is the topic of the Jacques Roumain œuvres that we have chosen. In the two novels, "Governors of the Dew" and "The Enchanted Mountain" and in news of The Prey and The shade, are reconstituted two worlds where the teenage Rouman grew. On one side ("The Prey" and "The Shade") lies the world of the rich mulattos and intellectuals kid bourgeois without true social project, on another side (Governors of the Dew and The Enchanted Mountain) lies the mountain villages where peasants without light lived, prisoners of routine, overwhelmed by their poverty, misery and agony.6

The social transformation consists in an effort to modify a situation and give it a favourable sense, to modify a situation of imbalance to establish a balance. An attentive reading of the writings (poems, narrations, news, and novel) of Jacques Roumain reveals us that the romantic reality reflects this imbalance, an imbalance of the Haitian social reality. In his works, the novelist undertakes the transformation of his society. The poem "New Negro" sermon makes a call on the Negro to recover and to rebel against the oppressing strengths.

We won't pray anymore
Our revolt rises as the scream of the storm bird
Above the flap rotted of the marshes
We won't sing the sad desperate spiritual anymore
Another song springs from our throats
We open out our red flags Stained of the blood of our just Under this sign we will walk Under this sign we will walk Standing the damned of the earth

The challenge of conscience and the revolt that is demonstrated in "New Negro" sermon is a departure from the contemplation and the resignation seen in the poems "Insomnia", "Black" and "Quiet".8 The hold on conscience evoked in "New Negro" sermon sees itself of advantage in the poem "Salt Negro." Here it is a rebuttal. Rouman affirms that the Negro does not accept to be the dirty Negro anymore.

> that the Negro
> don't accept anymore…
> to be your niggers your dirty Negro…
> because we will have chosen our day the day of the dirty Negro
> of the dirty Indian of the dirty Hindu
> of the dirty Indochinese of the dirty Arabic
> of the dirty Malaysian of the dirty Jewish
> of the dirty proletarians
> And has us up
> All damned of the earth all Justicierses
> Walking on the assault of your barracks and of your banks
> as a funeral torchlight forest to finish some
> one time for all
>
> with this world of Negro
> of niggers
> of dirty niggers9

"The Enchanted Mountain"-a peasant narration presents us a society overwhelmed by misery. The village is poor, the chalky earth cracks as the peel, the harvest is not worth anything. The night passes and gives up, abandoning him. melancholy thrives above ground, The day is only the certainty of long hours of laborious and bitter struggle in the torrid heat with the glebe rebels10 come the curse that attacks the children and the beasts also. After the drought, rain falls all day and the harvest is spoiled. Anguish weighs on the village.

Conscious of their misfortune the villagers meet to look for solutions. But it is an ignorant world. This ignorance is bound to the traditional practices of the village. However the collective conscience in a traditional community has a tendency to resort easily in an absolute metaphysics every time that it is confronted by a new, unexpected phenomenon".11 For the villagers it is the sorcery that brings this misery, therefore the solution resides in the murder of an old woman and her daughter (The supposed witches.) Here Jacques Roumain shows us that the social transformation is not achieved through ignorance. Murder is a brutal and inhuman action from the inability to understand that the drought is a natural phenomenon probably resulting from the deforestation of the landscape.

"The Prey and the Shade" prefaces a bureaucrat's life and depicts a corrupt society, hypocritical, abjectly bourgeois, that breaks the intellectuals but which the Haitian mulattos perfectly synthesize. For the mulattos all goes well, but Michel, the intellectual, feels torn from the inside. Joy envelops him at the time of his return to Europe, but five years later, he is incapable of adjusting to society. Life doesn't have a sense anymore for him, but he surmises, "I hugged the strong life too well. I seized it, stuffed it."12

His inability to find a solution to this conflict makes him hate his mulatto stepmother who on the contrary synthesizes this society perfectly. This hate returns him to the tolerable life. He tries to preach the like indigenised Haitian elite but it does not amount to much. He sees himself as a failure irritated by life. His past accentuates because he fails in politics. He writes some manifestos of poems and a novel and there again it is a failure because no one reads them. However he will get rid of this bitterness with life as soon as he accepts the place offered him, thanks to his stepmother. He believes himself to have passed the level of sheep of pasture, yet his dreams remain carried out. In being carried away by his cowardice, he gives up courage but demands it of his society that he hates so. Roman demonstrates here that cowardice is not able to anything in the transformation of a society whatever it is.

The second news "unattended" shows the intellectuals very conscious of the problem of their society but only attempt to analyse it. Daniel, a physician, feels the same way with the prostitutes in the suffering and the daily disgust, in his impotence and his cowardice before life. Jean, his friend and lawyer, provides him a good advice it is necessary to react. Yet they have everything necessary to succeed. In Haiti, to succeed means to be lawyer, engineer, physician or worse politician, to win the affluence to provide to eat well, to have an auto and to be member of the circle".14

But Daniel's sharp conscience makes him see such satisfactions as examples of an animal consciousness. The middle (course) makes it incapable to succeed at his way. In Haiti, as soon as a man looks for the right way out, gone is one sheep of pasture, he is treated like a black sheep...15

Poet Emilo on his own part does not write anymore, having always met indifference for all the encouragement. Jean notices that what is missing in the Haitian intelligence is a discipline which cannot be bent, which means to stretch stubbornly toward a goal. Where to find this discipline? In politics? Unlikely, because in Haiti homeland is the sum of interests that collide and repulse themselves. Is this not the African country picture?

Although these intellectuals know that a regenerative feedback will bring some solutions they let themselves go languishing in sadness. Feeling forsaken and useless, life remains a burden that weighs on them and makes them bend increasingly downward. They want to transform the society but the in the middle of a resistance give themselves over to frustrations.

The third news "The Jacket" is about two victims of the conscience crisis. Savire, who is confirmed psychopath by his labelled life of anguish and suffering, feeling pierced, tear-patched like his jacket hung on the wall, hangs himself. Some other part sees itself as another intellectual, who came back after a stay abroad he leaves his family. He enjoys a pension, but does not pay his rent; he writes some verses and read a heap of books. Then one finds him hanged.

This time to die is for them the only possible exit because they cannot solve the conflicts between their lives and their dreams. The social transformation doesn't achieve itself only by problem definition. Research and the adoption of the aimed solution are necessary. While presenting us these characters of the sharp conscience, Rouman prepares us for his hero, the leader, and the oppressed liberator.

The book Governors of the Dew, contrary to what we see in the other works goes farther. There is, first, an ignorance of the problems of the society: the drought, misery, the desolation, and the hostility. Life for the peasants may be penitence; there is no consolation. Himself is a believer abandoned by God. The peasants resign themselves and offer some sacrifices to pacify the divinities. Then Manual arrives, full of the experience of the laborious life that he had led in Cuba and conscious of the misery. He has a crisis of conscience, which pushes him in search of solutions. Courage doesn't elude him. He undertakes the struggle against ignorance.

In "The Enchanted Mountain" "The Prey" and "The Shade" one could not achieve a social transformation because of ignorance and lack of courage. Manual undertakes his people's education thus. It is not God who abandons the Negro, it is the Negro that abandons the earth and he receives his punishment: the drought, misery and the desolation.16

> Resignation is traitorous; it is the same with the discouragement that breaks you. Rosary in one hand, one waits for miracles and providence, without attempting anything.
> One prays for rain, one prays for the harvest, one says the prayers of the saints and loa. But providence it is to want the Negro not to accept the misfortune, to tame every day then the bad will of the earth, to submit to the caprice of the water with his needs, the earth calls it: dear master, he has other providence there that his serious inhabitant work, of other miracle that the fruit of his hands.17

He also tells them that the Negro is poor, unhappy, and miserable because of his ignorance.

> We don't yet know that we are a strength. Only one strength. All inhabitants, all Negro of plains and the glooms will be united one day when we will have understood this truth we will rise to a point as have the rest of the country and we will make the general meeting of the governors of the dew. The great union of the workers of the earth to reclaim misery and to plant a new life.18

The social transformation requires unity. Hoffmann (1973) commenting on the first revolt of slaves that succeeded (revolt in Saint-Domingue which became Haiti) noticed that it is in their unity that the success of the project is made possible.19 Manuel knows it well because he also undertakes the reconciliation of two hostile camps of Fund-Red. He has faith in man's capacity. Therefore he doesn't discourage himself before the apparently impossible task of finding water. It is his mission and his duty.

> The expérience hit him as the blind man's stick, and I learned that
> what counts is the rebellion, and the knowledge that the man is the
> baker of the pie.20

Finally he finds water. With the help of Anaïse, the news spreads. However Anaïse on the direction of Manual undertakes the education of his neighbours on the importance of water. Pursuing the movement for reconciliation, Manual surrenders to the meeting of the hostile camp. He explains to them what is necessary to bring water to the village. The malevolent Gervilen kills him shortly after. Christiane Conturie (1992) examining the reason of the death of Manual, remarks that for a Jacques Roumain faithful, political liabilities and strengths are first located in the society. Jacques Roumain, she continues, presents, from the gesture of Gervilen, the weight of the hate of all those that the success of Manual generates.21

Stephen Alexis answering the question: Who is Gervilen? Says that he was the symbol of dictatorship on Haiti, one of these ambitious men, jealous of all successes of the humble, these men incapable of regular work for the good of the whole.22

Before dying, Manual gives his will:

> If you warn Hilarion (agent of police) it will be once again the same
> history of Flavor and Dorisca. Hate and vengeance between the
> inhabitants. Water will be perdue…hurry to find Larivoire. Tell him
> the will of blood that flowed: the reconciliation, so that life restarts,
> so that the day rises on the rose.23

The inhabitants organise and construct the channel and bring water. Life is born again and the society is transformed. What is therefore the contribution of this display of the social transformation in Jacques Rouman's œuvre with the countries of Africa? Jean Paul, Satre (1948) tells us that the work of art is value because it is first a call.24 J.M Dash (1978) said that for the Haitian novelist the novel should be a kind of sociological investigating of society which would eventually reveal universal truths of the human condition.25 For Sartre (1948) does the writer speak for his contemporaries, for his compatriots, for his brothers of the race or class?26 As a consequence, the Roumanian œuvres are they not intended for Africa and for the countries of the third world? What country of Africa doesn't look nowadays like the Haitian society which Rouman depicts in these œuvres?

Africa today is marked by poverty, misery, suffering, ignorance, illness, violence, war, injustice and all abuses and vices of which one can imagine. Nwokora (2000) says that Africa remains the most upset continent of the world...Nigerians (as the other Africans) believe again that they have arrived as soon as they can buy a villa London or Paris and can live as the blank spaces in a document. [27] The mass of the African people as their accomplices in the Jacques Roumain œuvres are overwhelmed by misery, they lead a laborious life, a life like a slow death. The leaders and the politicians in the countries of Africa in their tower lead a life deprived of social conscience. They are corrupt and hypocrites. They marginalize and break the people's will.

Therefore a social transformation is required before this regrettable condition destroys the masses of the countries of Africa. We need a grasp of conscience of the socio-political problems of Africa as Jacques Roumain preached in these works. This grip of conscience would be followed of a conscience crisis. But Rouman shows that the two are not able to achieve anything without a regenerative feedback. Rouman agrees with Malraux (1946) who says, I don't like the humanity made of the contemplation of the suffering. [28] In addition to the grip and the crisis of conscience we need courage, the education of the masses. Therefore a strong confidence in human nature and the progress of which she is capable, the unity, solidarity, the collectivity of action, a reform of the people's morals and an economic reform by the means of agriculture.

The unity among the citizens even among the countries is unavailable in the social transformation in Africa. Nnolim (1992) affirms that the lack of unity among Africans results in the tragedy of Things *Fall Apart* of Chinua Achebe. On the other hand he continues, Sembene Ousmane in *God's Bits of Wood* demonstrates the obvious happy result when the masses of Africa's oppressed workers – men, women, children – uphold the conscience, with solidarity, collective will, and faith in man's capacity, which takes the form of an epic victory.[29]

The masses of Africa must wake up from idleness and sleep due to their cowardice. The contemplation of the suffering, misery and anguish in which we (the masses) drown does not serve any purpose. The solution of the socioeconomic problems of African countries does not reside either in emigration to Europe or the United States. One can earn his livelihood better as the Haitians made it in Cuba. But the future of these emigrants is not at all assured because while aging they become less and less capable to sustain the servile works that most of them undertake. It is necessary that we rise and fight against all oppressing and repressive powers that make our life a slow death. Let's teach the Red Fund villager.

According to Frantz Fetlock (1969) inter-African solidarity needs to be factual solidarity, solidarity of action, a concrete solidarity in men. African unity is a principle from which one intends to achieve a United States of Africa.30

The Roumanian objective to be his people's lawyer would be seen later among the writers as Richard Wright, Peter Abrahams, and Sembene Ousmane etc are maybe inspired by Jacques Roumain. In a word, through the presentation of the social transformation in his œuvres, Rouman carries the interest of the present political and socioeconomic problems of Africa. The display of steps towards the social transformation in these œuvres proves to be unavailable in the countries of the Third World so that the masses come out of misery and the poverty that threaten to crush them.

Chapter Five

The Feminist Impulse

F.I.Mogu

SINCE the advent of time and civilization, females have confronted what they perceive to be the male domination of affairs in the human society. According to the African-American feminist critic, May Helen Washington, all facets of the society must conform to the male order before they are adjudged to be correct. However, she reasons that this scenario cannot continue since it is lopsided and punitive of women. She argues for a fairer, egalitarian, non-sex biased society which accords similar rights and privileges to its male and female members alike. In her essay, "The Darkened Eye Restored: Notes Towards a Literary History of Black Women," she opines that:

> What we have to recognise is that the creation of the fiction of tradition is a matter of power, not justice, and that power has always been in the hands of men mostly white but some black. Women are the disinherited.... Those differences and the assumption that those differences make women inherently inferior, plus the appropriation by men of the power to define tradition, account for women's absence from our written records (Gates 32).

In *The Sexual Mountain and Black Women Writers Adventures in Sex, Literature and Real Life*, Calvin C. Hernton supports Washington's views and proceeds to show

104

clearly that the male domination of all aspects of life in the society still exists. He reasons that "the complexity and vitality of black female experience have fundamentally been ignored" and that, "black male writing has been systematically discriminating against women" (Hernton 39).

The situation referred to by Washington and Hernton reveals itself in the societies projected by Lucy Dlamini and Sembene Ousmane in Swaziland and the French speaking regions of West Africa respectively. Like in the African-American setting, women begin to emerge from behind the veil of male-based culture to voice their needs and concerns. Initially, they are taken for granted. Conversely, as events unfold, men begin to take them serious and to contend with their yearnings and aspirations.

Dlamini's *The Amaryllis* is set in Swaziland in the late 1960s and early 1970s. It also forays into neighbouring countries like South Africa, Botswana, and Lesotho. The title of her novel recalls a beautiful, pink-coloured, and sweet scented, but rare flower that grows from a bulbous plant found usually in semi-arid areas. Ousmane's God's Bits of Wood on the other hand, is set in the late 1940s largely in Mali and Senegal, two prominent regions in the former French West Africa. It is essentially about the strike action embarked upon by African workers on the Dakar-Niger Railway Line which spanned thousands of kilometres across different time zones, territories, peoples and cultures. Put simply, "God's bits of wood" means 'children of God the Creator' (Ousmane 62).

Dlamini's novel is about Tana Tanethu and other members of the Mdluli family in their quest to build a strong, economically sound and united family amidst the social chaos and decay of moral values in the Logoba / Mhobodleni / Ka Khoza area resulting from the rural to urban migration and the mushrooming of squatter settlements. These settlements were occasioned by the quest for wage employment at this period in the history of Swaziland, which threatens their efforts. *The Amaryllis* equally celebrates the establishment of the University of Swaziland fondly referred to as "Mvasi" and the warm reception accorded it by the Swazi nation. Historical figures such as the late King Sobhuza II and Professor S.M. Guma, accord the story some verisimilitude. Thus, the novel is a mixture of fact and fiction, credible and incredible events. The book therefore recalls works such as Felix Mnthali's Yoranivyoto and manifests affinity with *God's Bits of Wood* in the sense that, as Ousmane's novel recalls and celebrates the 1947/48 Workers' strike the Dakar Niger Railway Strike which outcome uplifted African workers and restored some of their dignity which had been denied them by the French Colonizers. In *The Amaryllis*, we witness a young woman making choices and determining her future. Viewed against the backdrop of her culture, the heroine of the story appears to be rebelling against the status quo.

Whereas the heroine in Dlamini's novel is Tana, in Ousmane's book it is Penda and a host of other women who ensured the success of the worker's strike embarked upon by their male folk. Penda led the African women on a long, arduous protest march to Dakar ,the French colonial Capital. In the course of the march and in the entire process of the strike, she was assisted and envisioned by other women like Dieynaba, Ramatoulaye and even the little Ad'jibd'ji and the blind Maimouna.

In *God's Bits of Wood* as in *The Amaryllis*, the events unfold over a vast canvass or landscape. The canvass in Ousmane's work is wider and larger than that in Dlamini's book. However, key activities occur within selected locations in the two texts such as Dakar, Thie`s, Bamako, Manzini and the University of Swaziland premises at Kwaluseni. The central point however in the two works is the emergence of the heroes and heroines who actively champion the cause of the ordinary downtrodden people in the society. In this case, we are looking at ordinary women who through dogged determination, commitment and discipline emerge as leaders and spokespersons of their various groups.

The renowned African writer, Ngugi waThiong'o argues in his book of essays, *Home Coming*, that "the artist must be part of the national struggle" (Ngugi xv). A relevant artist employs his art to educate the present generations of people while charting the future for them. The above ideas are also central in Ousmane's *God's Bits of Wood* and Dlamini's *The Amaryllis*. Ousmane portrays a colonial society undergoing transition. The colonized African people of "French West Africa" realise their innate power and potentials through group action. Through the 'Railway Strike, they realise that they could effect a change for the better in their lives. Prior to the strike, many of them did not believe that group coordination of efforts could result in a change for the better in their conditions of living. Dlamini on her part, paints a vivid picture of an emerging nation the Kingdom of Swaziland, with a population that eagerly welcomes the establishment of its premier academic institution the University of Swaziland owing to the people's enthusiasm for knowledge acquisition.

The dominant narrator through whose eyes we witness events in *The Amaryllis* is Tanethu Mdluli Tana for short. She is the first child and daughter to the Mdlulis. She is an ambitious, disciplined, intelligent, ideal and likeable personality that is also naïve in some instances. Tana is dutiful and completely devoted to her family and to her studies. In the University she falls in love with Reuben a fellow student but refuses to sleep with him. She believes that sexual consummation should come after marriage. Reuben however proceeds to date Sylvia and, in the course of the relationship, impregnates her even though he is not willing to marry her because he believes his real love to be Tana.

Although the society depicted in the story seems to turn a blind eye on Reuben's lack of responsibility over Sylvia's pregnancy and plight, Tana faces a dilemma as she cannot understand why a young man who claims to love her, but has put another lady in the family way and abandoned her in the process, still wants her to marry him. Tana is determined to climb to the top of the academic and career ladders. She is resilient and does not experiment with casual sexual relationships as her younger sister, Zakhe and her bosom friends and schoolmates. She is resolute in her convictions about dating a single man and avoiding sexual intercourse until after marriage. This stance deprives her of her first and only boy friend, Reuben who is impatient to the point that he experiments with a willing girl. Tana's position is at odds with the prevailing trend in the Swazi Society so vividly depicted. She believes the trend to be morally reprehensible. She thus wages a relentless war to sensitise her siblings at home and her friends at school against such a practice. Her posture which stands against the predominant male ordered ethos surrounding her, is credible and realistic, but appears strange and weird in the existing social parlance. However, she is the voice of reason, a visionary whose actions and beliefs serve to warn against the consequences of promiscuity as manifested in the contemporary society. Tana Mdluli is therefore a suitable role model for today's youth in our HIV AIDS' devastated world.

In *God's Bits of Wood*, a strike situation involving local African workers demanding equal labour rights and fairer treatment from their French Colonial employers serves to mobilize and enlighten both men and women to united action and team work against their oppressors and exploiters. For instance, it is during the strike that, contrary to their traditional role as housewives, women are allowed to attend and address a political meeting in a society where the very idea is "unfamiliar and disturbing." We therefore realise "how many traditional beliefs are being swept aside by the turbulence of the strike" (Wilfred 178).

The Dakar-Niger Railway Strike brings about a situation where men become increasingly dependent on women:

> The days passed, and the nights. In this country, the men often had several wives, and it was perhaps because of this that, at the beginning, they were scarcely conscious of the help the women gave them. But soon they began to understand that, here, too, the age to come would have a different countenance. When a man came back from a meeting, with head bowed and empty pockets, the first things he saw were always the unfired stove, the useless cooking vessels, the bowls and gourds ranged in a corner, empty. Then he would seek the arms of his wife, without thinking, or caring, whether she was the first or the third. And seeing the burdened shoulders, the listless walk, and the women became conscious that a change was coming for them as well...And the men began to understand that if the times were bringing forth a new breed of men, they were also bringing forth a new breed of women (Ousmane 53-54).

Penda a fearless female organises a march with other women in support of the Workers' Strike. She subsequently emerges as a foremost leader of the march by African women from Thie's to Dakar. In the course of the strike she makes a speech at one of their meetings. The speech confirms her leadership status:

I speak in the name of all of the women, but I am just the voice they have chosen to tell you what they have decided to do. Yesterday we all laughed together, but for us women this strike still means the possibility of a better life tomorrow. We owe it to ourselves to hold up our heads and not give in now. So we have decided that tomorrow we will march together to Dakar (254 -255).

The Amaryllis depicts a situation where the protagonist, Tanethu Mdluli's unique personality emerges. Her male friend, Reuben takes her out to the lawn for a chat soon after they meet at the University. In the course of the chat we observe her resolute position on issues such as dating and courtship. Reuben ventures thus:

'Tana,' ...'I would like to know you better, and maybe you and I could be friends in a special kind of w...' However, Tana responds: 'Not so fast Reuben, ... 'we scarcely know each other yet' (Dlamini 70)

At this point, Tana patiently listens to Reuben a he intimates her with his family background. Once in a while she interjects to elicit more information from him. It is only when he has finished telling her his background that she responds fully by letting him know about her. When, much later, Reuben raises the issue of pre-marital sex, Tana resolutely opposes the idea. Tana's other name is Busisiwe which literally means "we are blessed to have you" (57). Therefore, she must live up to her billing. At the start of her University programme, her parents emphasise this point to her:

'My child, Tana,' Father said, turning to me, 'your mother and I don't know how to thank you for being such a blessing to this family. You have truly lived up to your name, Busisiwe "we are blessed to have you" which your mother gave you. Your mother and I feel truly blessed for having such a child.'

'We also trust that you'll continue to heed our advice while you're at that place of higher learning, which we have been warned, can destroy a child morally. Also, do not forget to read your Bible.'
'So, my child, … we, in turn, will keep you in our prayers, beseeching the Almighty to keep you on His straight and narrow path (57- 58).

This parental advice and exhortation further strengthens Tana's convictions about her future and her leadership role both in her family and in the larger society. Hence, in her rapport with friends and schoolmates, this resolute commitment, which seems to be solitary in her neighbourhood, stands out conspicuously. It also sustains her when Reuben, her boyfriend, attempts to blackmail her into engaging in pre-marital sex with him through his carnal and superficial relationship with Sylvia a girl adjudged to be wayward. Tana's bosom friends and school mates, Julie and Patience try to persuade her to revise her stern stance regarding casual sex, but she remains committed to her resolution against it. Julia admonishes Tana:

'You know, Tana,' … 'I wouldn't be your true friend if I didn't give you my honest opinion. Reuben loves you, and I've not the slightest doubt that if you revised your stand on certain expectations in a relationship between two people who love each other, he would dump that ntji…'
'No, Tana. I'm telling the truth. Reuben's using Sylvia for what he can get while waiting for you to change your mind (94).

However, Tana does not change her attitude or waver in her tough stance. She instead sulks and devotes all her energies to her studies in a bid to surmount the emotional set-back:

In the succeeding days and weeks, I felt as conspicuous as an aching tooth, knowing that most people were aware that my

111

relationship with Reuben, begun with such promise (though Bemona, the malicious would call it pride) had been nipped in the bud. To stifle the pain I buried myself in my books, deriving deep satisfaction when each assignment was returned with nothing less than a B grade and very warm comments from my lecturers. At weekends I escaped to my home to breathe fresh air. Meanwhile, Reuben himself had kept his distance since the Sunday following my discovery. After church he had approached me but I had frozen his steps in mid-stride by hissingly telling him to get lost. And from then on, I never looked back. I was disillusioned and bleeding inside, but I refused to give either him or the onlookers the satisfaction of seeing me waver. (98)

In *God's Bits of Wood*, Penda's speech at the strikers' meeting in Thie`s energizes other women into positive action as they decide to march to Dakar to vent their anger and frustration at the French Colonial exploitation of African workers. It is even acknowledged that, "it was the first time in living memory that a woman had spoken in public in Thie`s,..." (255). Ibrahim Bakayoko who is viewed as the 'strength' and 'soul' of the strike, lends firm support to the women in their planned march. Bakayoko and Lahhib are regarded as the 'soul' and 'brain' of the Dakar Niger Railway Strike respectively. Bakayoko tell the other strikers:

> 'We have no right to discourage anyone who wants to strike a blow for us,' he said brutally. 'It may be just that blow that is needed. If the women have decided, all that is left for us to do is help them. I move that the delegates from Dakar leave immediately to warn the local committee of their arrival... (255- 256)

True to Bakayoko's reading, the march from Thie`s to Dakar proceeds and succeeds. It thus becomes the lethal blow which serves to alert the French Colonizers to the firm resolve of the African Strikers to attain their objectives of having all the demands met. The solidarity exhibited by the women in their march to the colonial headquarters strengthens the strike and adds fervour to it. The workers refuse to return to work under the old working conditions and the strike drags on and degenerates into what Hadrame the shopkeeper describes as "a war of eggs against stones" (65). The authorities cut off supplies of food and water in a desperate and cruel attempt to force the strikers back to work.

In the resulting hardships and confrontation with agents of the colonial authorities, many people lose their lives. Those who survive suffer untold hardships that extenuate their endurance and this brings out the worst traits in some individuals, while it also reveals the best, but hidden attributes in others. Still, the workers remain adamant and the strike lingers on. In the end they win as the French Colonial Railway Company accedes to the Strikers' demands. A foremost leader of the Strike, Lahbib, sends a telegram from Dakar which confirms the end of the Strike: "Conditions accepted. Strike terminated. Return to work tomorrow..." (320).

It is plain that, whereas in *The Amaryllis*, Tana Mdluli is a moral voice for Swazi women on crucial social issues that affect all women, Penda and other females in God's Bits of Wood actively join their menfolk in an economically driven battle against colonial, capitalist exploitation to regain dignity for Africans. In the process the women break new grounds as they begin to make themselves heard and felt poignantly in public meetings for the first time in their society. Dlamini's novel voices opposition to some long-established, male-based practices in the Swazi society as exemplified in the responses of the heroine, Tana to these manifestations, while Ousmane's book shows African women in a colonial and exploitative situation pooling their energies and ideas together to wrest the initiative from their foreign oppressors as a step towards redefining themselves and charting the future for oncoming generations regarding the usefulness of team work. To corroborate the story, Ousmane remarks in his Author's Note on the Dedication Page of the novel:

> The men and women who, from the tenth of October, 1947, to the nineteenth of March, 1948, took part in this struggle for a better way of life owe nothing to anyone: neither to any "civilizing mission" nor to any parliamentarian. Their example was not in vain. Since then, Africa has made progress (v).

History has revealed that Ousmane was among the strikers. Even though the story is told with some fictional undertones in a novelised form, the strike did occur within the dates stated above. And, the African strikers won a sweet victory which serves as a lesson till today. Ousmane's statement above serves as a backdrop to the revolutionary import of *God's Bits of Wood* and goes a long way to give the Railway Strike much credence and place it within the framework of a historical milieu. The author employs this propitious historical framework to present exemplary characters and pursue nearly all of his favourite themes of anti-exploitation, anti-colonialism and pro-Africanness (Pan Africanism) themes espoused and propagated by the Negritude Movement. Ousmane is therefore an Africanist who is fully committed to the ideals of black consciousness or the beauty of the African cultural heritage.

A close reading of *The Amaryllis* reveals that, like Ousmane, Dlamini equally cherishes and advocates this Africanist consciousness. Accordingly, she projects key characters in her novel who set the tone for other people to follow. For instance, she vehemently condemns and renounces some emerging tendencies the renegade western habits of

114

loose living, casual attitudes and the appropriation by females of male clothes. These are practices that run counter to the traditional African heritage of closely-knit family subsistence. As Tana Mdluli is ready to depart for further studies at the University, her father remarks:

> While I cannot say all daughters should follow their mothers' examples, at least I can ask you to do exactly that. My child, don't like your prodigal sister, deprive us of the joy of one day giving you away in marriage to a deserving young man, and of presenting us soon after with grandchildren, all begotten within a marriage sanctioned by the church. I, therefore, ask you to keep away from all those alcohol-drinking and cigarette-smoking young men.
> 'This country is changing before our eyes. Certain behaviours that we thought belonged to big cities like Jozi or Thekwini have now been brought here. For example, I have even seen some of your age mates walking around in trousers. Again, we don't expect you, once you are out of our sight, to begin dressing like a harlot. Trousers belong to men. Why indeed should women want to wear trousers when we men never long to be seen in a skirt?'
> 'So, my child, I don't expect you to defile your father's house by coming here wearing trousers. You are not a man nor have I seen any indication of the harlot in you ....' (Dlamini : 58).

Ousmane and Dlamini employ literature to propagate their cultural ideals. Dlamini's heroine, Tana remains steadfast throughout the story. She heeds her parents' advice. Ousmane's females led by Penda energize their menfolk with a supportive protest march from Thie's to Dakar in their bid to ensure a successful strike. Both writers harness history by recreating action and recalling events which occurred in the past to spur other generations to follow the appropriate paths by making the right choices in life. Essentially then, the two texts act as vehicles for far-reaching and progressive social change. The characters in the two novels embark on a journey of change for the better in their various societies.

Chapter Six

Ngugi's Marxist Aesthetics

MSC Okolo

THE core of Marxism can be located in the primacy of matter over mind. For Marx and Engels, it is the economic that governs and defines the basis of every relationship. In the 'Manifesto of the Communist Party' Marx and Engels (51) aver that man's consciousness changes with every change in the conditions of his material existence in his social relations and in his social life.

Existence, clearly, precedes consciousness. Man's material well-being determines the degree he can take part in other activities. A person who is hungry, unsheltered, and naked, apart from being a liability for the society, will hardly have time to engage in any extra-economic venture. His primary concern will be to meet his basic needs.

In a class society, such as engendered by capitalism, the struggle between the owning but nonworking capitalist class and the working but non-owning proletariat class can only be resolved through political revolution. While the economic is the most crucial factor determining every relationship, political revolution is the only workable means of bringing about a change in a class exploitative society.
The most desirable social condition will emerge when the state withers away and communism is instituted.

Marxism is surely teleological; it aims at transforming a given society. According to Marx (30) 'the philosophers have only *interpreted* the world, in various ways; the point, however, is to change it.' This change can only occur by transforming the mode of production of material life, which alone determines the general character of other processes of life.

No doubt, for Marx and Engels, literary and artistic developments are determined by the mode of production of material life the economic structure which ultimately always asserts itself on all other activities. All the same, although it is the base that determines the superstructure, the degree of interaction Marx allowed between them suggests that the superstructure can influence the development of a society. In a class society, where a dominant economic class ends up with determinate political and economic influence in all spheres of the society, the law is unlikely to be reflective of the interests of the underprivileged. Equally given that a writer is a member of the society, he cannot be separated from its antagonistic class relationship. He can through his work offer critical appraisal of the existing political situation and this way can mould or redirect his society's actions, beliefs, ideals, values, and ideas. This way ideas contained in literature can influence peoples' perception about politics and the best means of effecting a political change.

Since a writer lives in a given environment and belongs to a class, he cannot be neutral. A Marxist aesthetics offers a choice for a particular artistic production over another. According to Ngugi (38), there have been two opposing aesthetics in literature, 'the aesthetic of oppression and exploitation and of acquiescence with imperialism; and that of human struggle for total liberation.' Marxist aesthetics is in agreement with the latter. It helps in the evaluation of economic relations, which ultimately plays a decisive role in the political and ideological struggles in the society. Balibar and Macherey (3) observe that 'class struggle is not abolished in the literary text and the literary effects which it produces'; rather, 'they bring about the reproduction, as dominant of the ideology of the dominant class.' Marx and Engels (51), indeed, assert that the ruling ideas of each age have ever been the ideas of its ruling class.

A Marxist aesthetics, then, helps to show that it is within the province of art to portray the possibility of men to struggle against all obstacles. 'From the standpoint of the revolutionary,' so says Omafume Onoge (44) 'the political criterion of excellent art is art which serves the struggle of the people against their oppression.'

Ngugi's (Marxist) Aesthetics

The central sense Marx understood aesthetics, also, it seems, applies to Ngugi who sees literature as 'a reflection of the material reality under which we live' (96). The writer's primary responsibility in Ngugi's view is to channel his creative energy towards the production of the aesthetic devoted to the fight for freedom, exposing the distorted values integral to capitalist exploitative system and the struggle against exploitation in a class society. To carry out this task, a writer has to be sensitive to the class nature of the society and its influence on the imagination.

Literature is part of the class power structures that shape our everyday life (Ngugi xii). A writer's works invariably reflect the various struggles political, cultural, ideological and economic going on in the society. Every literature is a commitment to a particular political ideology and every writer is a writer in politics (Ngugi xii). For literature to be meaningful it has to assume a revolutionary stance. Its focus must be on a critical appraisal of the economic structure of modern society, which is essential in getting a revolution going. Ngugi's ideal is for a literature that is committed, assertive, confrontational, which can bring about a more equitable change in human relations, especially, in the unbalanced relationship between the West and Africa and other third world countries. Truly, literature is teleological; its goal must be to transform a given society.

In this sense, the essential task of literature, at least for the African writer, is to act as a vehicle of liberation from European imperialistic capitalism, which has placed the West at the core and Africa and the third world at the periphery in economic and social relations. It is only a revolution that can restore to Africa and its people the self-image and confidence necessary for the radical transformation of society. Literature cannot stand apart from the social processes taking place in the society. Its thoroughly social character makes it partisan; literature takes sides especially in a class society (Ngugi 6).

For this, the African writer must shun 'abstract notions of justice and peace' and actively support the 'actual struggle of the African peoples' and in his writing reflect 'the struggle of the African working class and its peasant class allies for the total liberation of their labour power' which alone provides the foundation for a socialist transformation of the society (Ngugi 80). In Ngugi's summation, Marxist oriented literature is the aesthetic viable for the future and the only literature worth producing by the writer.

The Example of Petals of Blood

Ilmorog, the setting of most of the major social and political activities and a typical representative of a post-colonial African society, was once a thriving society with a huge population of sturdy peasants before the advent of colonialism. With colonialism came a number of changes. European farmers robbed the farmers of the virgin soil they needed for shifting cultivation. Trapped in farming and re-farming their small exhausted acreage with poor implements, their production declined drastically. The youths that could have helped in the farm were lured because of better facilities to work on European farms or big towns.

In any case, the introduction of taxes by the colonial government further acted as a push for the people to sell their labour to European farmers in order to earn the required money, which they could no longer raise through their own sterile farm. So what they earn through their labour-sweat (which is barely enough to keep them going) they give back to the government as tax. In essence, their material condition instead of improving was only made worse. Instead of their earning to make it possible for them to be able to break free of their European Masters, it made them completely dependent on them. On the other hand, their old parents left at home were reduced to the barest subsistence level farming, which equally compromises their former production status as independent producers.

Events revolving round Ilmorog also point to neo-colonialism as a key factor in the decline of African societies. For Ngugi (24), neo-colonialism means the continued economic exploitation of Africa's total resources; Africa's labour power by international monopoly capitalism through sustained creation and maintenance of subservient weak capitalistic economic structures, captained or supervised by a native ruling class.

Nderi, the MP representing Ilmorog and the quintessential representative of the African leaders that emerged after independence, shows no difference from the exploitative attitude of the colonisers. He adopts their ethical code of 'greed and accumulation' (163). Ensconced in the capital, he completely forgets the place he is supposed to be representing. His whole attention is taken up in enriching himself and ingratiating himself with the West. He accepts offers of directorships in foreign-owned companies. And diverts the money he collected from his constituents for a water project as a security for further loans to enable him buy shares in companies, invest in land, in housing and in small business.

Next, he forms the *kiama-kamwene* cultural organisation (KCO) with few friends to ostensibly 'bring unity between the rich and the poor and bring cultural harmony to all the regions' (85). The poor are forced to take an oath (tea drinking) that will protect the riches of the few. The tea drinking is, of course, not free. The poor are tricked cum forced to pay twelve shillings and fifty cents. And these are people 'threatened by lack of water; lack of roads; lack of hospitals' (85) and whose means of sustenance is to scratch a fatigued earth. The loot collected from the 'Mass Tea Drinking' exercise goes to make the few rich people even richer. Nderi's share runs into millions.

There are other sides to KCO. In reality it serves to strengthen 'progressive cooperation and active economic partnership with imperialism' (186). Nderi sees it as an avenue to create wealthy local economic giants as exist in the West. It is also made to act as the 'most feared instrument of selective but coercive terror in the land' (186). It is employed to eliminate political opponents and suppress any resistance from the peasants and workers. Far from acting as a forum for cultural harmony, the KCO is used to ensure that nothing is allowed to upset the economic, social and political gap between the super-rich and the super-poor. Commenting on this post-independence development, a character in Petals laments:

> this was the society they were building: this was the society they had been building since independence, a society in which a black few allied to other interests from Europe, would continue the colonial game of robbing others of their sweat, denying them the right to full flowers in air and sunlight (Ngugi 294).

By the time the Ilmorogians are forced by severe drought to trek to Nairobi to make their plight known to Nderi, he has become one of the richest MP's in the land. He owns 'a huge farm in the Rift valley, a number of plots and premises in Mombasa, Malindi and Watamu, shares in several tourist resorts all along the coast' (174) and many more lucrative business interests and connections. All this, while the community he represents can effectively be described as 'a deserted homestead, a forgotten village, an island of under-development which after being sucked thin and dry was itself left standing, static, a grotesque distorted image of what peasant life was and could be' (184). The trek, however, makes Nderi realise the need to 'develop' the area. In the end, Ilmorog is transformed into a 'modern' town, thanks to Nderi. The trans-Africa road that links Ilmorog to many cities of the continent 'was built, not to give content and reality to the vision of a continent' (262) but to pander to the recommendations of foreign experts. The Utamaduni Cultural Tourist Centre was set up as a camouflage for illicit business in gemstones, ivory, animal and even human skins. It also acts as a recruitment centre for women and young girls as slave whores from Africa. The New Ilmorog Shopping Centre attracted the development of wheatfields and ranches, which displaced the herdsmen. Banks, tourist centre, brewery,

123

churches, whorehouse, all compete in the 'scramble' and 'partition' of Ilmorog. The residential areas also mirror the different class interests. The Cape Town is for the rich; 'New Jerusalem' a shantytown of migrants and floating workers, the unemployed, the prostitutes and small traders is for the poor. This, invariably, is where most former Ilmorogians end up.

So in ten years of the journey to the city, Ilmorog peasants had been displaced from their land: some joined the army of workers; some became semi-workers, working both in a plot of land and in a factory; some turned to petty trading in hovels and shanties that did not belong to them along the Trans-Africa road, or criminals and prostitutes. The few who tried their hands at making sufurias, karais, water tins, chicken-feeding troughs; shoe-makers, carpenters are pushed out because of stiff competition brought about by more organised big-scale production of the same stuff.

The events in Ilmorog lead Karega, through whom the political ideology and artistic vision is enunciated, to probe the root cause of the problems and also to search for the solution. He discovers the underlying cause in imperialist capitalist economy that ropes people in a new kind of slavery and neo-colonialism. According to him, 'a man who has never set foot on this land can sit in a New York or London office and determine what I shall eat, read, think, do, only because he sits on a heap of billions taken from the world's poor' (240). Kwame Nkrumah (ix) notes that the 'essence of neo-colonialism is that the state which is subject to it while possessing outward trappings of international sovereignty is in reality dependent' for the reason that 'its economic system and thus its political policy is directed from outside.' For Ngugi (45), monopoly capitalism (and its external manifestations, imperialism, colonialism, neo-colonialism) 'whose every condition of growth is cut-throat competition, inequality, and oppression of one group by another,' is what has disfigured the African past. What system, then, will end the exploitation of labour by capital? How can imperialist capitalist economy be fought and overthrown? What system will 'free the manacled spirit and energy' (50) of African people so they can build a new united society? So then, what will free African workers from economic servitude and thereby guarantee Africa's genuine political emancipation?

Karega finds the solution to the imperialist impasse in the alliance of the workers and peasants to carry out a radical socialist transformation of the society. For him the key to creating a 'more humane world' in which the inherited inventive genius of man in culture and science is put for the use of all lies with the poor, the dispossessed, the working millions and the poor peasants equipping themselves with guns, swords and organisation, to change the conditions of their oppression and seize the wealth which rightly belongs to them. Certainly, 'imperialism: capitalism: landlords had to be fought consciously, consistently and resolutely by all the working people' (344). As a matter of fact, 'tomorrow it would be the workers and the peasants leading the struggle and seizing power to over turn the system of all its preying, bloodthirsty gods and gnomic angels' so as to bring 'to an end the reign of the few over the many' and 'only then, would the kingdom of man and woman really begin, they, joying and loving in creative labour' (344). In *Petals*, there is a pronounced aesthetic of resistance, commitment and ultimate liberation.

Limits of Marxist Aesthetics

Marxism is a 'theory of the nature of history and politics as well as a prescription for revolutionary action to bring the industrial working class to power and create a classless society' (Daniels 388). The only workable solution to the persistent economic crisis that torments capitalist economies and the oppression of man by man that characterises human history is worldwide socialist revolution. For Marx (51), man's consciousness changes with every change in the conditions of his material existence. And at certain stage in their development 'the material forces of production in society come in conflict with the existing relations of production' and 'then occurs a period of social revolution. With the change of the economic foundation the entire immense superstructure is more or less rapidly transformed' (67-68).

The end point is to create a society in which huge discrepancies in power, wealth, material possessions, opportunities, privileges, and, especially, private ownership of property are abolished in order to achieve justice and equality which are the basis of guaranteeing cohesion, harmony and fairness in the society. This is only possible in the higher phase of communist society. In this final phase of communism, the enslaving subordination of the individual to the division of labour, along with the antithesis between mental and physical labour will vanish; labour will cease to exist for monetary rewards but become life's principal need; and the productive forces will increase with the all-round development of the individual, and all the springs of co-operative wealth flow more abundantly. At this point, society can inscribe on its banners: 'from each according to his ability to each according to his needs!' (Marx 263). That is, the state has disappeared 'withered away' and a 'classless' communist society established.

Communism at its philosophical core, then, 'amounts to a belief that man could not fulfill his humanity unless society was transformed so as to liberate him from all individual acquisitiveness' (Kyung-won 17). Without doubt, 'man could obtain true freedom only through the absolute destruction of all structures of inequality' (17).

But what is the implication of offering Marxist revolutionary stance as the best means of resolving Africa's political impasse?

To start with, the workers-peasants revolt may not be as inevitable as Karega strongly upholds. The teleological assumption that history has a purpose that will inevitably culminate in the destruction of capitalism and the establishment of communism is not irrefutable. Marxism is premised on the economic circumstances acting as the base supporting all other institutions whether political, legal, artistic, and, even, military. Since this is the case, a revolutionary attempt by the poor working class is most likely to be frustrated by a circular dilemma. Which is: for the property-less exploited workers to effectively carry out a revolution, they need to secure the economic base. And since they do not have the economic base, they cannot carry out an effective revolution. Besides, there is really no good reason to suppose that even if capitalism has some inherent weaknesses that they are enough to lead to its disintegration.

Again, Karega's position entails that people would think the same way on important matters; that there is a panhuman nature common to all people; and that class antagonism is certain. In *Petals* Nyakinyua's attempt to organise the dispossessed of Ilmorog into a protest to fight for their land ends in some of them deriding her. Those whose lands are not to be auctioned off refuse to get involved. This suggests that, possibly, the working class will be more prepared to work

127

within capitalism through reformist methods, than to fight for its abolition. Jules Townshend (251) points out that 'the working class ideologically has tended towards reform rather than revolution.' Robert Daniels (394), equally, observes that in countries (such as Britain, Scandinavia, the United States, Canada) with rising living standards and democratic access to political power, Marxism has never had more than a limited and passing appeal; and it is hard to apply the Marxian theory of proletarian revolution, however interpreted.

Given that Marxian revolution has failed to take place in highly industrialised and capitalist economies as Marx, indeed, believed, it might equally not work in Africa. There are, in fact, good grounds for this proposal. Marx's model of two antagonistic classes does not really exist in Africa's political experience. So class politics in Africa cannot be reduced to a simple competition between bourgeoisie and proletariat (Thomson 91). For instance, in Nigeria, and indeed in most African countries, the poor standard of living of most people is such that by all reasonable criteria should have pushed them to the brink of revolutionary violence, yet nothing of the sort has happened. Instead poor people actively support and canvass for the rich, especially, during elections. They can even go to the extent of fighting each other for the sake of their 'man'. Those who do not express themselves in this way are, often, more interested in finding ways to accommodate themselves to the hard conditions instead of channelling that energy towards a revolution, which they view as unprofitable.

Even supposing the poor working class in Africa embark on successful socialist revolution, it is unlikely they will sustain it once their condition changes. Far from advocating for a socialist revolution, most labour unions in African societies are more interested in securing better working conditions for the workers. It appears *Petals* underrates man's basic disposition. This is: when people gain greater knowledge they may disagree on the meaning of the rules they previously adopted. Man is most likely to change under different circumstances.

Besides, there is a problem lurking in the simple assumption that once workers become the leaders all disagreement will melt away. There is an equal possibility of workers not automatically buying the ideas of their revolutionary leaders. It is also not impossible that extra-economic considerations difference in national identities, religion, and gender can play important role in shaping the economic. Karega discovers in the course of his wanderings that male workers denigrate the female ones; those from the same linguistic enclaves and clans and regions tend to bond; while some workers easily give up everything for their religion. In Nigeria, for instance, ethnicity and religion are as much a cause for civil strife as, if not more than, economic problems.

Moreover, there is no good basis to take for granted that the worker-peasant alliance that will act as the driving force that will topple the capitalist system must materialise. It is plausible that the different groups may end up mutually suspicious and antagonistic of each other. Again, it is possible that exploiters will emerge among the workers. Robert Daniels' (390) points out a major weakness in the inner logic of Marxism as 'the question why the dialectic should stop once capitalism has been overthrown; why not a new ruling class exploiting the masses on some new basis?'

Moreso, for a system that has taken centuries to develop as in the case of capitalism, it may well be naïve optimism to assume that it will quickly disappear. Arthur Ripstein (287), observes that the end of the historical inevitability of socialism was attacked for being 'unscientific, for denying the role of human choice in history, and for conceptual confusions about the relation between individual and society.' Francisco Weffort (99) sees the future of socialism to achieve a new meaning and make a corresponding political comeback in the admission that 'socialism, in any imaginable form, should be understood as a possibility rather than as a historical necessity.'

Also the feasibility of the new world of freedom and prosperity that will be ushered in under a communist system is not without some difficulties. To bring about a communist system will entail some degree of serious conflict between capital and labour. Ryan (401), rightly, notes that at the point where 'the "solution" to the problem of a more equitable distribution of the rewards of economic cooperation becomes the destruction of one party to the competition, politics ceases and civil war begins.' This evidently is not the kind of environment that will encourage prosperity, or even, freedom. The defeat of capital will, most probably, put labour on the alert so as to suppress any insurrection. Moreover, it is really not the case that once someone is a worker or poor, then, he must be the exploited and if someone is rich, then, he is an exploiter. Really, there is no such a neat divide between employers and workers. There are instances where workers are also employers. Abdulla started out as Wanja's employer before they became partners. Even peasants are known to employ labour during cultivation and harvesting. It does appear that Karega's narrow and strict presentation of orthodox communism cannot guarantee the broad field of culture and expression needed, even, for communism to survive.

Yet, it will be a mistake to write off Karega's proposal. By highlighting the shortcomings of capitalism, he unveils an undeniable truth. Which is that where the worker is alienated from the product of his labour, he is likely to become resentful and this can lead to a violent revolt. This situation will invariably destabilize the society as the worker views it as hostile instead of being the means of his self-realization.

Ngugi's approach has contributed significant dimensions to the analysis and understanding of African politics by showing that dependency of African societies is partly imposed from the outside. Through centuries of exploitation of the resources in Africa the West is able to establish poverty among African societies. It is this that has turned African societies into continuous 'receivers' of the crumbs that fall from the 'masters' table. The prime obstacles to the national development of African societies are the colonial heritage and the unequal international division of labour.

Given that the West needs the collaboration of African leaders to maintain this status quo, the only way to overhaul the system is through a socialist revolution that will weed out leaders whose interest are aligned to the West. According to Ngugi (84) why there was no real change after independence was because 'the African bourgeoisie that inherited the flag from the departing colonial powers was created within the cultural womb of imperialism.' Nkrumah (xv-xx) notes that the rulers of neo-colonial states derive their authority to govern, not from the will of the people, but from the support, which they obtain from their neo-colonialist masters. He goes further to observe that 'the less developed world will not become developed through the goodwill or generosity of the developed powers,' but rather only through 'a struggle against the external forces which have a vested interest in keeping it undeveloped.' To struggle against imperialism and its comprador allies is to struggle for a truly human civilization.

A Kenyan research on the activities of Multinational Corporations (mnc) discovered that 'mnc investment distorts industrial growth in poor areas, and confirms their dependence and underdevelopment, rather than promoting the widespread effects of genuine development' (Langdon 12). Foreign interest in Nigeria's oil is the major factor that drew attention away from thriving groundnut, cocoa and other agricultural products. The result: 'Africa's leading oil producer now has the third largest number of poor people in the world' (Wallis 34). For Ngugi (96), 'no country, no people can be truly independent for as long as their economy and culture are dominated by foreigners.'

In addition, by emphasising the adverse effect of foreign domination in the political terrain of African societies, Ngugi exposes the biased perspective of modernization theories. The modernization school believes that the only way African societies can achieve rapid development is to follow the western capitalist path, preferably that of the United States. Communism under this consideration is a threat to modernization of African societies. By pointing out another threat imperialistic capitalism Ngugi provides an alternative for a more balanced criticism. Indeed, *Petals* makes a strong case against inherent vices of imperialistic capitalism the exploitation of the majority by the privileged few, the erection of money as the criteria of all values, extreme individualism, tyranny of one class of society over another, inordinate wealth accumulation by a few at the expense of the majority.

Furthermore, by highlighting the negative impact of imperialistic capitalism, Ngugi shows why, even, effective democracy and human right programme do not succeed in African societies. Poverty makes it easy for people not to resist corruption and other vices, which militate against the institutionalization of democracy. Wanja prefers to become a prostitute than to 'return to the herd of victims' (Ngugi 294) - like Abdulla who is reduced to a roadside fruit seller. Ngugi

(83) sees imperialism both in its colonial and neo-colonial stages as the 'one force that affects everything in Africa politics, economics, culture, absolutely every aspect of human life.'

To this point, another may be added. What Ngugi wants appreciated is that development is an integrated whole covering physical survival, economic survival, political survival, cultural survival and psychological survival. For African societies to pursue a meaningful development, there is need to completely destroy Western dominance. In Ngugi's conception of society as a complex in which politics, economics, and culture are inextricably tied up, capitalism cannot offer hope of progress and social justice that can be said to be accessible to all (Ikiddeh xiv). Essentially, the point for Ngugi (xii) is: for African societies to achieve a fundamental social transformation that is required, there must be a real break with imperialism because 'imperialism and its comprador alliances in Africa can never develop the continent.'

Besides, Ngugi's sense of outrage at the disparity in wealth, power, and well-being between owners of productive property and the actual workers is understandable. Daniels (389) credits the ethical appeal of Marxism as a creed of equality and fraternity as a major factor in its political success. In *Petals*, Inspector Godfrey, although an ardent believer in the sanctity of private property, still realise that the 'system of capitalism and capitalistic democracy needed moral purity if it was going to survive' (334). Existence of socialist nations provides a challenge for capitalism and checks its activities. For Ngugi (19-20), a modern Africa can only emerge from a true national culture that 'nurtures a society based on co-operation and not ruthless exploitation, a culture that is born of a people's collective labour.'

Moreover, there is worldwide outcry against capitalism. Joan Baxter (32) reports that the first-ever Africa social forum meeting held in Bamako early in 2002, with participants from 45 African countries, was directed at industrialised countries and their financial institutions which dictate the policies that make African governments so unpopular with their people privatisation, structural adjustment, open markets and cutbacks in social services. Some of their slogans read: 'Down with the World Bank! Down with the IMF! Down with neo-liberalism! Another Africa is possible!' Baxter quotes Ahmed Ben Bella, Algeria's father of independence, who led the protesters as declaring: 'Today in Bamako, we are burying capitalism.' Baxter also quotes Aminata Dramane Traore as dismissing the claim of the World Bank and IMF that they are leading the fight against poverty in Africa. As far as she is concerned 'they are producing poverty. They just maintain themselves by making money from the poorest.'

The African activists also rejected the New Economic Partnership for African Development (Nepad) developed by the Presidents of Nigeria, South Africa, Senegal and Algeria. Their grouse is that it was developed without the participation of civil society and may well not be better than the ones imposed on Africa by the West. Chris Simpson (39) reports that 'some of Nepad's detractors argue that it does nothing to challenge the supremacy of the North and the weakness of the South' instead 'Nepad meekly follows the received wisdom of the IMF and the World Bank, courting the private sector and embracing globalisation at whatever cost.' To be sure, international support is required in the three fields health, education and poverty alleviation which are of special importance to Nepad. Tony Blair visited Africa Nigeria, Ghana, Sierra Leone, Senegal early in 2002 to support Nepad which he calls a new partnership between Africa and the developed world. Yet at the G-8 summit in June, 2002, in Kananaskis in Alberta, Canada, Nepad's representatives hope of securing a growth rate of seven percent of gross domestic product with an annual US$64 billion in public and private investment was dashed. The 'G-8 Africa Action Plan' issued June 27, 2002, instead, pledged to provide additional funding to make up a US$1 billion shortfall in debt relief owned by African nations; and for each G-8 country to determine its own level of aid to Africa in accordance with her respective priorities and procedures. This, of course, is on the condition that African nations could prove that they were serious about fighting corruption. It does appear that the critics of Nepad have good grounds for their cynicism especially if one compares the 'crumbs' Africa received at the summit against the $20 billion the G-8 spent to assure the dismantling of nuclear warheads in Russia.

To conclude, Daniels suggests that the significance of Marxism should 'be weighed as a contribution to the development of modern politics and social thought rather than as a dogma that must be condemned or taken on faith.' (390). By studying the contemporary African political situation within a socio-economic context, Ngugi cautions on the need to be wary of what is taken as development. Importantly, he provides insight on how to recognise change; what is to be regarded as progress; and a warning that the world is changeable the exploited classes can through a revolution bring an end to their exploitation. Indeed, Petals functions as an instrument for conscientising; it reveals how the revolutionary class stands in relation to other classes materially and historically.

What is more, Ngugi's submissions will remain relevant so long as capitalism is unable to solve the problem of neocolonialism, dependency, underdevelopment, poverty, wars, debt crisis, ecology, global inequality, massive corruption, violence, rigging of elections, bribery, erection of money as a standard of all values, lack of basic infrastructures, famine, water shortage, and the like, that are affecting contemporary African societies. To end on Claude Ake's remark: 'what socialist theory questioned was not the productivity of capitalism but its sustainability in the face of the contradictions that it engendered.'(33)

Chat Forum

Chapter Seven

Functionalism in African Literature

GMT Emezue

with Ossie Enekwe

"When I was in the university, most of our lecturers sounded as if we didn't have drama in Africa. Eventually when I got to the United States I came in contact with drama works from other parts of the world. I saw Japanese and Chinese drama. But above all (I saw) how drama was presented in Japanese culture for instance.

Furthermore I studied history of drama and I realised that my teachers were wrong in supposing that we don't have drama in Africa. They felt that the dances which were ritualistic in nature lacked dramatic impetus because they believed that ritual and theatre were opposed to each other. But this was only the Western concept of drama which does not pertain to other cultures..." – *Enekwe*

Q: PROFESSOR, you are a renowned critic and scholar of dramatic literature, as well as a creative writer of several poems and fiction. I suppose it will be proper to set the mood of this interview with a rendition of one of your poems.

Ans: Alright. I will read from the collection *Broken Pots*. The poem is "To a friend made and lost in the war: in memory of Martin Utsu."

God had saved you

From escaping in the purple flow.
But you had too many holes.
So you died among strangers.

We could not find you.

1

At Ihiala, Ozubulu
And Eluama where you lay
On the tracks of enemy guns.
But a hungry driver
And a tired truck
Hauled you into a ditch
In a thick bush.
Blood oozed from your nose,
Mouth and ears;
And at a village hospital
Where they nursed you
"God may get tired
Of saving me," you said
To me, a smile on your lips

Two days later
Soviet bomber rockets
Burst your belly
And tore your intestine
On the white sheet
Of the hospital bed.
They must have been

They bore you weeping
To another place
And tried to stitch you,
To keep your soul

Q: Naturally, the question that would follow such a moving rendition may be "who" and "what." Specifically, who was Martin Utsu and what was your relationship with him?

Ans: I was in the Biafran Army during the Nigeria-Biafra war. At that time I was in the Propaganda Section. Martin was from Ogoja, Itigidi, that is the present Northern Cross River. He was one of the men in the group I headed. There was this young girl from Akwa Ibom and she and Martin were to get married. We all used to interact. You know, just as people do until suddenly, Martin dies. And that was that.

Q: I find the elegiac note quite powerful; it resonates rather strongly of the African dirge sentiment you explored in "The Story of a Ceylonese girl" which I studied extensively in my book where I had remarked on circumstances for philosophical reflection on the tragic phenomenon (Dirge 110).

Ans: In fact the first time I realised the power that this poem had over people was at Columbia. My course mates and I used to present our poems to each other. One day when we were out on a boat trip. We were yet to set off and one of the girls from Ireland suddenly caught my hand and said: "This poem is powerful; each time I read it I cry. It is almost as if I could see the whole thing happening." There have been other instances where people remarked on the power of the poem. So since that time I realised that the poem is quite touching.

Q: Funso Aiyejina once described your poetry as belonging to the 'generation of broken promises' who formed the Odunke community of artists' with chap books 'Omabe' and 'The Muse' as means of expression. What was your relationship with these groups?

Ans: Well, I was never a member of Odunke group of artists. But many of their members were my friends. I supported their activities, but I was never a member. Around that time I was very busy I was appearing on television as guest artist at Ukonu's club along with Sunny Okosun. The rehearsals and performances kept me very busy.

Q: What would you think was your greatest influence in your writings? And apart from the war are there other factors that influenced your writing?

Ans: Yes. The war influenced my writing all right. But the fact was that I was writing long before the war. But with war experience something happened to me. For the first time I became more aware of life. I realised that life is precious and should be treasured. I realised that life should be valued. There were many wastes during that war and the human waste was the greatest. I began to perceive life in a different dimension. Also when I travelled outside the country, I became more aware of what was happening. I became exposed to things going on around the world. I read other writers like Pablo Neruda, Ibsen etc. I also interacted with other writers like Amiri Baraka who was a close friend. So, all these acted as sources of influence on my writings. For instance my other collection of poems *Marching to Kilimanjaro* reacts to other issues in Africa.

The other one *Gentle Birds* is a collection of poems which could also be enjoyed by adults as well as children. I subtitled it 'for the young and young at heart' so I wrote it so that adults can enjoy it too (*Reads from the collection*).

Q: In an interview, you observed that 'it should be possible for the artist to create in such a way that the reader is able to participate in what the writer is talking about'. In the search for a functional aesthetics, can the choice of language limit or enhance the realism of his art?'

Ans: Of course, it can. The diction affects the work. I feel that a writer in his use of language should aim at how to reach his audience. Language should express the action. You allow the character to say what they want to say. You know you just present the character to the audience and the audience interacts and judges the character. You know the writer does not judge his characters for the audience.

Q: How then would you describe the readership in Nigeria?

Ans: Very poor. Nigerian readership is very poor. But then it appears the writings that go on reflect the quality of reading one has undergone. The youths can no longer pick up a book and read. They are not interested. They don't have the time to read. They only read just to pass exams and nothing more. This has seriously affected the type of leadership that we produce nowadays. I think it might also have something to do with teaching. I remember when I was in secondary school. We had one teacher Mr. Hart, a very articulate man who taught us in those days. He used to read out lines/portions of the literature book for us in class. Through he told a lot of stories but the way he handled the teaching made us become every interested in the subject. For instance when we read *Treasure Island*, he would come to the class and read: "One stormy nights…" All these attempts laid emphasis on aesthetic aspects of the language.

Q: Have you had a cause to review your work for technical reasons?

Ans: No hum… I will just say that I enjoy reading many of my books. I also do a lot of editing on my works. I have poems that I wrote over ten years ago, which I have not yet published because I am still going through them. I am very careful before I present my work to the public. So far I have not received any such reactions.

Q: Unlike some other books based on Biafran experience, one has noticed an attempt to change names of characters in *Come Thunder* though it is obvious that most of these events happened in Biafra.

Ans: Immediately after the war people didn't want to talk about Biafra. Long after the war, one of my classmates kept calling a 'rebel'. I told him that I was not a rebel. But I noticed that they were so concerned with what I was doing at school then. Apparently we were held in suspicion. I believe that the poor reception of some of my books in other parts of Nigeria is because of the ethnic differences in the country. Take for instance my book *Come Thunder*, when it was presented to ANA, they only gave me 'special; mention'. But even that 'special mention' was done in a funny manner. Where my names should be, they put only 'Ossie' leaving off the surname. Under the column for Book Title, they wrote 'Come' only instead of 'Come Thunder'. But abroad many critics were talking about my short stories and poems. So in the long run, my experience has been that once something is about Biafra, the story or work will not be well received in Nigeria. So in a way, that was why I changed the names of the characters. Also, within fictional bounds with the change of name of characters and setting, I was free to stretch my imagination to any scope. If I had adhered to factual names, I will feel constrained to stick to facts. So I believe the change served dual purposes.

Q: A reviewer of *Come Thunder* dismisses it as paying 'little attention to details of description' and what she calls 'lack of deftness' in portraying the characters in the book. Buchi Emecheta, at the turn of the century lamented that African novels are not real novels because they are not as voluminous as those found in Europe. To you what makes an African novel?

Ans: Well, in my own view, it is not the size that makes a work a novel *per se*. Let's take for example a very small novel by Hemmingway *The Old man and the Sea*. This a very small book, but very heavily loaded. The European concept of novel will tell you about culture, about what somebody is wearing, the colour of shoes, eyes and so on. We have not developed that sense of elaborate details because the African by nature is not in the habit of elaborating and expatiating on things by giving unnecessary details. Sometimes we talk about social environment, interaction, and dialogue. I am aware of all these. And I believe that everything that was meant to be described in that novel was described. I don't think that review was justified. In fact I described everything in that book. I

143

don't know what other details that should have been added that was not done. (Reads a detailed description of environment and action on pages 38) I wonder what other description I should have added here without belabouring the point. As I said earlier, I believe the west (of Nigeria) didn't like *Come Thunder*. I am not surprised at that kind of review.

Q: You just pointed out that our novels are culturally influenced. Does this make the African novel inferior to their foreign counterparts?

Ans: No. As far as I am concerned, our novels are as good as any in the world. When I was growing up I didn't even like bulky novels. The aesthetic elements have nothing to do with size.

Q: What prompted the writing of *Igbo Masks: The Oneness of Ritual and Theatre*?

Ans: When I was in the university, most of our lecturers sounded as if we didn't have drama in Africa. Eventually when we started reading something by (Ruth) Finnegan who had done a lot of work in the area of African oral literature, many of the lecturers and scholars were repeating the same thing. I actually doubted what they were saying. When I got to the United States I came in contact with drama works from other parts of the world. I saw Japanese and Chinese drama. But above all how drama was presented in Japanese culture for instance. Further I studied history of drama and I realised that many of my teachers were wrong in supposing that we don't have drama in Africa. They felt that the dances which were ritualistic in nature lacked dramatic impetus because they believed that ritual and theatre were opposed to each other. But this is only the Western concept of drama which does not pertain to other cultures. By the time I went to the U.S. to do my doctorate, I spent a lot of time thinking about this. My special authors were Shaw, Steinberg, and O'Neil. In fact I thought I was going to write my thesis on Shakespeare. But because of the realisation I had concerning our own drama, I decided to research into this. When I went to my supervisor and told him that I was researching into Igbo Masks, he asked me 'What was that?' I told him that it was African Theatre. Initially he was doubtful if such a thing actually existed. Fortunately, around this time a group from Yale theatre advertised for papers in African Theatre and I sent in a piece which they published. In fact when I was taking the book to my supervisor, I was afraid because I was not sure what his reaction would be. But he was excited and encouraged me. He was impressed. In fact what I am going to say now will buttress the point I made as far Yoruba and Igbo are concerned. Even in deciding to write on this Igbo theatre, I was sent to the department of Anthropology. The practice in Columbia then was that if a substantial part of your work falls into another discipline, a professor from that discipline will need to be part of your supervisory team. So they asked me to go and talk to a professor in the Department of Anthropology to see if he would l join the team. I took it for granted that the professor would agree. But when I called him and told him "Prof, please I am writing my thesis on Igbo Masks," he said "Yes, I know you very well. What has that got to do with me?" and dropped the phone. I picked up the phone and called him again. He said "Are you taking my course in anthropology?" I said "No." He dropped the phone again. Then in the evening a young Yoruba saw me and said that the Prof said he was in a bad mood when I called him -that I should call him again. But when I went to my supervisor he advised me to keep clear of the man. The man has already shown that he was prejudiced. So I had to find another prof, this time, a white and he was quite happy to supervise me.

Eventually, when I finished writing, my supervisor had to cancel his leave to be present for my defence. It was during that occasion that it was decided that the work will be published. It was sent to the university press. The first reader praised the book highly. It was sent to the second reader who happened to be the same prof. His attack on the book was very personal. Eventually I had to abandon the idea of publishing the book abroad. Later I was told that Prof. Skimmer, the disgruntled prof, worked for Nigeria during the war and was anti-Igbo. He didn't want to hear anything concerning the Igbo.

But another interesting incident happened during the publication of the book at home. The manuscript was sent to Prof. Adedeji, the oldest professor in drama. He said that the status of the book was marginally acceptable. But by the time he was making this recommendation, the book had been accepted for publication by the *Nigeria Magazine*. He recommended the book reluctantly and also recommended that I should be marginally promoted. I didn't know what was happening at that time.

But the University of Nigeria policy is that alternative opinion be sought when there is an unfavourable recommendation. From Prof Adedeji's recommendation he was saying that he was not sure whether *Nigeria Magazine* would publish the book. It was only later that the faculty discarded his recommendation and asked another professor's opinion. And this Professor gave high scores. But Prof Adedeji had not scored me for that book and I wondered why. It was much later when the editor of the *Nigeria Magazine* saw me that I got to know what was happening.

I didn't even ask before he blurted out about how Prof. Adedeji had come to query them why they should accept my manuscript for publication. He told them that he was the oldest professor in theatre arts and he had a number of papers for publication too. "Please accept my papers" he had said. But the editor told him that his request could not be granted. The prof kept phoning and later took his complaint to the director of the publishing house. The director said to the editor: "Prof Adedeji is the oldest professor in theatre arts. Why do you not want to accept his papers?' The editor replied" "It is not that we do not want to accept it, but we already have our budget covered."

At that time they had agreed that they would accept one work from North, West and East respectively. So they had no choice but to publish the book. Otherwise they would have killed *Igbo Masks*. So that is how the fight has been. They have been fighting the book, but unfortunately the more they fight, the more popular the book becomes. They have been fighting *Come Thunder* too. Because you know that in *Companion to African Literature* edited by Douglass Killam and Ruth Rowe, *Come Thunder* is mentioned there. Under the section "West Africa" (Prof Enekwe reads) '...like the poetry the prose explores various themes without showing any radical ideological or technical inclination by the writers. Igbo writers explore such issues as the anti-Igbo pogrom in Northern and Western Nigeria the direct cause of Biafran secession, Biafra's heroism... post war habilitation. Representative examples are S.O. Mezu's *Behind the Rising Sun*, Chinua Achebe's *Girls at War*, ANC Aniebo's *Anonymity of Sacrifice*, John Munonye's *A Wreath for the Maidens*, Flora Nwapa's *Never Again*, Buchi Emecheta's *Destination Biafra*, Cyprian Ekwensi's *Survive the Peace* and *Divided we Stand*. Ossie Enekwe's *Come Thunder* is a book in the manner of Thomas Paine's *The Red Badge of Courage*' (end of reading). You know that *Red Badge of Courage* is a very short novel but very powerful. He compares *Come Thunder* with *Red Badge of Courage*. When I saw this I

147

was happy because *Red Badge of Courage* also inspired me in writing my novels.

Q: Your book has indeed triggered off waves of similar explorations in other cultures like Ibitokun's *Dance as Ritual Drama and Entertainment in the Gelede of Ketu-Yoruba sub group of West Africa.* Coming back to the idea of masking, I will like to put back to you the question you asked at the end of *Igbo Masks* but in this way: What has been the experience of Igbo Masking and theatre in the face of prostitutionalised entertainment?

Ans: Let's start with our Ivory Tower. Our so-called intellectuals are so obsessed with perpetuating European forms. They don't understand that these have very drastic and dangerous effect on everyone for the fact that you are not promoting your own drama tradition. So the unfortunate thing now is that the young ones are growing up not knowing that there are indigenous forms that can compete with European forms. They believe that the only form that is really worthy of attention is the European form, because even your colleagues don't seem to understand what you are talking about. They see it as an intellectual matter. They don't see it in terms of promoting indigenous drama which has the potential of bringing wealth to the country. I mean if you start a very good traditional performance group, it can bring in tourism. There was a time we started masquerade performance in the old Anambra State. I was a member of that committee. There is a video of most of the performances and at the beginning, it was very successful. But our academics feel differently. They feel that performance is just something for the paper. You put it there and it ends. But it is something that is meant to be practised regularly. We are not saying that we should have the same religion as our grandfathers. We don't have to have the same religion. But the mask, the idea of mask is quite universal. This *Adamma* and her daughter going around for instance, I used to tell my students that if we get just one *Adamma* mask and her daughter (also masked) without doing anything but just walking in from the university gate, you know just walking. You will just have people following them. That is the way tradition and culture is. And if we follow drama based on masking, a lot of people will understand it. Even in my department, I just noticed that most of the courses assigned to me were in the area of African Drama, as if that was the only thing I read in the university. The others want to be identified with foreign things. But I am not bothered. I believe that this concept of drama could even be realised in the 'written' form. I did a play called "Dance of Restoration." Where I wrote it was in the United States when I was a scholar in residence. I see it is pure African Drama, full of dance. Even the rhythm expresses Africa. We performed it at Shell Camp, Warri, when they invited us. Unfortunately I have not had time to complete it as fully as I would like. I saw it as an example of modern African Drama where you have characters dancing normally as they dance. So that is the problem. What I would like to see is more and more people acting and reflecting African dramatic traditions like the Chinese drama. When you watch it you know that it truly reflects the culture and people it talks about.

Q: It is interesting to hear you mention another drama piece you worked on. I recall an interview published in *Weekend Concord* (1991), where you mentioned your drama piece 'The Betrayal' which was enacted at University of Nigeria. In that interview, you tagged your creativity in the drama genre as an 'experimentation' which aims 'to achieve a situation in drama whereby the word and action become one.' How has this 'experiment' been received?

Ans: What I mean is a drama where the character is not the author. It is not the character speaking the voice of the playwright, but the character speaking according to the nature of the performance. Not the playwright giving lectures through the character. Anything that is not connected with the action will be eliminated. It is not a law that a character must make long speeches. A character can just sigh. That will reflect exactly how he feels. I must also add that I was an actor. On one occasion a woman came from Britain and conducted an audition and I came out best. One of the things that struck them was that I wasn't talking much, unlike the other actors who were shouting and raising their voices to emphasise their anger. They were totally surprised. We were all given the same script and the people who had been performing in the Eastern Nigerian Theatre took the main roles. I came into it because I just said to myself 'let them allow me to do the role just once as they believed I was not relevant. We argued and argued and at last the young woman agreed. The script was the same and we were all meant to act the role. By the time I finished my act the white woman exclaimed: "Excellent! Excellent!" From that time John Ekwere started taking me seriously. So when I came in to Biafra to join the force at Aba they said there was an information group being directed by John Ekwere. I told him to help me get into the group. He said "Look, that's a waste of talent." This is because he had discovered that I was a good actor. He sent me back to the men in charge of the drama group. When I told the man that John wanted to see him, he asked "For what?" I told him that it was because I wanted to join the drama group. The man refused. So I went back to John Ekwere and told him what happened. John Ekwere was very angry with me. He said "What is wrong with you. Why did you tell him that it was about you?" But I had to tell the man the truth because I find it difficult to tell lies. That was how I lost out. I couldn't get into the drama group. But this is just to show you that some people were aware I had the talent for acting. In fact when I watch what is going on in the video film home movies (nowadays), I am ashamed I don't even want to watch what they are acting. The actor doesn't need to talk too much. In normal life you don't need to talk too much. Sometimes somebody says something you don't respond. It is even more dangerous. It shows more anger when you don't respond. But our people believe that when you shout it shows you are very angry. Of course *Betrayal* is not yet complete. It is one of the works that I am still trying to expand and get published. But essentially it is talking about corruption which has become one of the main issues in Nigeria today.

Q: You have partly answered the next question we have concerning your view in the recent proliferation of home video in Nigeria today. The impact of these new wave of entertainment in the development of our socio-economic values as a nation...

Ans: The problem is diverse. I won't blame the people who are doing this because of the inactivity of the so-called intellectuals. It seems that the kind of education we are given makes us more educated but more inactive. So if you look around most of the businesses are run by people who are not educated. Even in politics, people who are there are mostly illiterates. Because the educated ones, once they have finished, they pick up these white-collar jobs, sit around and imitate Europeans. So talking about people being practical with things, if you want to be a performer, you perform. Don't feel that because you are a university lecturer, you cannot go on stage. So coming what these people (home video practitioners) are doing...well, there is vacancy, there is lack of performance, nothing is happening, so they are filling a gap. And they are there now and it is difficult for you to penetrate -very difficult because the government is not interested. It is a very serious problem because they are transmitting a lot of wrong things that will take centuries to undo.

Q: Even in the perception of Nigeria by our neighbouring countries –the way they perceive us– because of this home video...

Ans: You see there is a lot of discrimination. Sorry to say that my experience has shown me that. I have done my best. When I started off I did my best. I formed a theatre group which I took round the schools in the East. We even performed in Umuahia. We went to Government College Umuahia where we did Macbeth. Do you remember those public performance of Macbeth in the 80s?

Q: Yes

Ans: I was there. I took the plays even to Owerri and Port Harcourt. We went to perform in secondary schools. Sometime, in 1984, I did *Trial of Dedan Kimathi*. That was the first theatre production in the city of Abuja. -a very successful production. But the press refused to talk about that production. That is what I mean by discrimination. Because if that production had been done by Yoruba performers, perhaps the news would have been everywhere. See, in 1993, I came back from United States of America and decided to take Nkpokiti dancers to the U.S. Before I returned to Nigeria, I had concluded with Brooklyn Academy of Music to sponsor the trip. Everything worked out well. I even wrote a brochure which was the last thing they expected me to do. But just when we were about to start off, some Yoruba took over. When we now got the letter from this people they said that our performance will only be in New York. But before then we had agreed that we would tour American cities. But you are dealing with people who don't understand the power of culture. Most Igbo don't understand the power of culture. So

152

you are alone when you are talking about culture because you are inadequate - unless you talk about modernity.

Q: Your direction of Ngugi Wa'Thiongo's *Trial of Dedan Kimathi* performed at University of Nigeria and University of Ibadan was highly praised by Ihekweazu and Osundare. In an interview you said that the director could be a creator.

Ans: Yes.

Q: How has this concept helped your stage directing and how do you think it will help the concept of directing in Nigerian theatre?

Ans: It boils down to what I was talking about indigenisation of culture. Somehow, when somebody is creating, the person is reflecting his culture, and the person is also reflecting himself. So somebody writes a play. That he writes a play does not mean that when you put it on stage it is going to be the same. In fact the play as written is different from the play on stage. That's the first assumption. Now, talking of culture, your culture, your cultural awareness should help you to determine the kind of staging; the shape you give to a production, a piece of drama. You know what your people like and what they don't like. I think that's where the creativity of the director comes in. You begin to adjust the work in such a way that your audience becomes satisfied. Not just to pick the work and put it exactly the way the author puts it. What I did in *Trial of Dedan Kimathi* was to move things around. I took one of the last scenes forward. At the end of such changes I noticed that the audience enjoyed the performance very much.

Q: If you were to direct *Death and the King's Horseman* with Wole Soyinka's pontificating that no attempt should be made to make this play look like a clash of culture, is it possible that this can be realised by the director with such a specific instruction?

Ans: It is his business to write a play as a playwright. He cannot pontificate for a director. If I take that play now and decide that instead of it being a Yoruba dance, it should be Igbo dance, he cannot stop it, heh? To the question of clash of culture and all that, of course there is clash of culture. Wole Soyinka is a problem in that sense, for instance when some Africans were talking of Negritude Wole Soyinka condemned Negritude. But Negritude was important. It was important because if you don't say "you are," nobody will say "thou art." This idea of saying that you are something is being carried out by Europeans all the time. So I disagree with Wole Soyinka in many areas. I think he is a powerful individual. But the danger comes when somebody starts to pontificate that this is the way things are. If you know the way, you think along that line but also you should allow other people to think in their own way.

Q: Let's look at *The Last Battle and other Stories*. Some critics had noted what they termed 'superficial treatment of female characters' in this book. It can be observed that your female characters are either depicted as being helpless, suffering, or being cheated and exploited by the men. And when they gear up to retaliate, they seem to shoot at the wrong target, like what happened in 'A Band of Amazons.' Does this reflect the Nigerian society or is it your own attitude or perception of women?

Ans: My own attitude to our women folk is that I recognise that they are exploited and I think in these works I merely draw attention to the fact that women are exploited. That is my main concern. And the way they end is not meant to be all that conclusive. It is a way of raising some questions. But saying the treatment is superficial (laughs) … we are talking about a specific period. What was the one you mentioned?

Q: 'Emente' and 'A Band of Amazons.'

Ans: That is a way of emphasizing the contradictions in the society. There is so much uncertainty. There is this other one where the girl jumps out of a moving car…

Q: 'Escape.'

Ans: Yes. I am trying to emphasize the vulnerability of women. I am emphasizing their humanity. The story 'Emente' is a unique short story. It was based on an actual experience and then I developed it. I don't think the case of Emente has anything to do with attitude of society. It has to do with ethnic factor because she was not Igbo; she was Efik and suddenly found herself abandoned in the hospital with nobody to attend to her. And in my youth, by that time I was about to enter the university. I had gone to see a doctor when I saw this lady. She had the Women Teachers College uniform. She walked into the place and she was collapsing. Eventually, they took her in to see the doctor. And I was curious; that type of curiosity that any young person would experience. So afterwards I wanted to find out whether she was okay. When I got there I was touched because the moment she started telling me about her condition, her helplessness, I could no longer escape. I could not abandon her. So I went to the hospital on some occasions to visit. I think I contributed to her survival because what happened, I had come to her and her mouth was closing. She told me that she had not eaten anything so I went to the gate of the hospital, where they have UNTH now and bought some eggs and then sliced the eggs and put into her mouth. So she was able to get something into her system. And before I left, the way she talked meant that she needed me there. She didn't want to be abandoned. She wanted somebody who cared to be close to her. I didn't know her; I didn't even know her name. So eventually I would go home and say 'I won't go to see her again.' But eventually my conscience would not allow me to rest. Then I would make ready and go see her. Then one day I went, only to discover that she had been discharged. Now if you wrote a story and concluded it with "She had been discharged," I mean, it won't have the impact. I continued working on it - whether it should be first person or second person, whether I should be saying, 'This young man did ...' or whether it should be 'I'. And then how should it end? I wanted it to end without saying whether she was alive or dead. That would be more dramatic. And that was what I did.

Q: Yes, most of the stories in that collection ended that way. For instance 'Handling the Enemy' and 'The Last Battle...' Even in *Come Thunder,* you are not told whether the hero survives or not. At the last scene Emeka is just charging and charging...

Ans: You are very perceptive. It is just a question of your aesthetic sense.

Q: Your instinct as a dramatist must have aided your writings...

Ans: Of course it did. For instance, as I was saying about Emente, I did not see her as often as I used to before she was discharged. I think what happened was that I was afraid she was going to die. I was almost scared. But one day when I was in the university, we had a big party. That time we used to invite bands from Ghana such as the Uhuru Dance Band to come and play there. That was when the students union was better organised and run by responsible people. So I was sitting with my friends during the party when someone came over to me and said a lady wanted to see me. I walked over to the table and the young woman standing there. She said: 'Do you recognise me?' I looked at her and shook my head. She now said: 'do you remember the girl that you helped at....?' I shouted in surprise. Indeed it was the girl at the hospital.

Now I was thinking of a name to give her in the book, I decided on 'Emente' because I believe the name will suggest someone from that area of Cross River. Not that this was her name, because I had forgotten her name. But I was happy that she survived. I believe I played a role in her survival because if I hadn't been there, who knows. Even my presence, even just visiting her must have helped her to survive.

Q: One also notices that most titles in that collection are ironical. For instance, in 'Escape' the heroine, instead of actually being free to live her life, 'escaped' into death' by jumping out of a moving car. Once again, 'The Last Battle' turns out to be the point of surrender for a very tough soldier...

Ans: (Laughs) ... Yes. The man surrenders. It is ironical alright.

Q: I wonder why the titles are like that. Does it point to some kind of artistic cynicism?

Ans: I think life is ironical. And irony is an artistic device, a powerful device because that is what the audience is never expecting.

Q: A few years ago Chinua Achebe felt that his role as an artist was to inform and educate his people. I believe that he did that successfully because whoever reads Achebe's works will come up with that sense of African pride and belonging. What would you like your readers to deduce from your works?

Ans: I think I am very much concerned with the issue of justice. If you read *Marching to Kilimanjaro* you will see this. I am a combatant and at the same time I feel deeply and this has an impact on my writing. Like some of those poems like "To a friend made and lost in the War," I couldn't have written it if I was not feeling deeply about the issue. And "The Story of a Ceylonese Girl" and there are other elegies. I wrote one 'To the memory of Nnabuenyi Ugonna." I wrote this poem 'In memory of Bernard Beckerman.' He was my supervisor in Columbia University. He died three years after I got my Ph.D.

It was very painful because he took me like his son. So it was a way of expressing my love for the man. (Reads from the poem)

> Gather the past about the bosom
> Cast in the breeze of bronze
> In cups of honey ...

It is the same poem that they published in the anthology that was put together for the man.

Q: Finally, let's look at your most recent book *Trails in the Mines* published 2000 by Minaj. This book is supposed to be a biography of Edmund Nwasike, the first Nigerian mining engineer and the first indigenous general manager of Nigerian Coal Corporation. But this book achieves more than this to become a documentation of early history of Nigerian Coal Corporation and social life in Enugu. Why did you adopt this style of writing?

Ans: Yes, as you have noticed, I went to great extent to show the socio- historical background of the events that occurred. How the colonial powers took over and the resistance they had from the various communities, and also to show the contradictions in the policy of the British. So I thought that it is not just enough writing a biography without showing the historical milieu in which most of the events took place. Most of the time I tried to capture the social background. That means that I had to do a lot of research to familiarise myself with that period. You know, instead of just writing a biography and just talking about the man because I know that one won't just understand the person without understanding the social milieu.

Q: In *Trails of Mines* I noticed that the story centred on coal mines. Could that be a source for the story 'A Band of Amazons?'

Ans: Well, yes. It was like an echo from 'A Band of Amazons' helped in *Trail of Mines*. People then were much more aggressive than what we have now, because people now are more docile, very docile. Nigerians are more docile now unlike in those days; because I remember. You know some of the things you remember, as a child will come into your stories whenever you find you are writing. When I was a little boy I saw women marching in protest. I experienced it. It became a way of keeping all that memories alive. Recollecting that incident when writing, the topic was so strong that it kept coming and the result is this 'Amazon'.

Q: Prof, what, briefly, can you tell us about yourself that brings to bear on your writings?

Ans: I don't know where to start with myself. But let me say this, when I was a child, I fought a lot. I fought. I wasn't fighting with my sibling. I fought outside the house. I fought not because I wanted something from people, but I fought whenever my right was denied me. For instance, when I was a child, I was very tiny and I found myself going to fetch water because Coal camp had no water that time. I would go with my bucket to fetch water at the pump. I found that very often bigger boys maltreated me. One day I brought my bucket. It was my turn to fetch water. We had to line up. So I took my bucket and put at the tap. Somebody bigger than me took my bucket and threw it away. Not just even pushing out my bucket, but he grabbed the bucket and threw it away. Then he ran. I was a good marksman. If I aimed a stone at someone, there is no escape. So as he was running, I picked a stone, aimed at his head, and threw. It hit him and blood started running. And some people started pursuing me, trying to catch me. I ran and ran. I didn't want them to take me to my father, because I was afraid my father would beat me for what I did. I knew that though I was fighting for my right, I had broken somebody's head in the process so I ran away. They took the young man to the hospital. Eventually the family of the boy came to our house and the matter was settled.

Another day when I was in primary school, we were doing this 'show me your whip.' You know what 'show me your whip' means?

Q: Yes. You agree with your partner that both of you must always carry a whip and when you don't show yours, you will be flogged.

Ans: Yes. So one day, I had my whip and this person came to me. He was taller and bigger than I was. He said 'show me your whip.' I showed him my whip. He snatched it from me, flogged me, and started running. I looked around, found a piece of stone, and threw it at him. *Kpo-o-o*! If you saw the blood coming out of his head, it was like a stream. The young man got a big stone and started pursuing me. I ran into Uwani and a woman was carrying oil with basket on her heard. I got the woman and turned her around as I ran around her. As I tried to escape, the oil fell on the street and the boy missed me. But they caught the boy. The blood was flowing too much out of his head. So people caught him and stopped the blood. And my teacher said: "*I gbu go nu ya nu, I ga akpo ya eje hospital.*" (You have killed him. You have to take him to the hospital.) So I took the boy to the hospital.

On another occasion, I was playing the masquerade. I was very tiny then but they used to call me 'Ossie Terror'. I was in front of the group. They were playing this ogene. You know, the ogene can make you do unimaginable superhuman things. So we were moving and there was this young man on the road. He refused to run like the others, because when the

160

masquerade was coming you were supposed to give way. But he stood there. Heh! Then I said (there were certain incantations that we used to recite that goes like this):

I na echem? I na echem?
Nkiri, nkiri ka-ana ekiri mmanwu
Ukwu ose anaghi ari ya elu.

(Translation)
Are you still there? Waiting for me?
You can only watch a masquerade (from a distance)
You never climb the (pepper) plant

After reciting this, I turned around to give time so that the young man would go away. My group was following me playing their ogene. Then when we turned back he was still standing where he was. And I said "I na echem eche?" I walked straight up to him and flogged him. In short we beat him up thoroughly. As this was going on, the police came and arrested all of us. That was during Christmas. They took us to that police station near the near the market. They asked us 'what went wrong?' We explained and at the end, they discharged us. That was one case.

In another direction, when I was a child, I had a good voice. At 11 years old, I was a member of the Holy Ghost Choir. We went to the Marian conference. At that age I could read music very well. Our choir master then was Reverend Fr Kelly, a white man. That one passed and I went into St Patrick's choir. I eventually joined 'Young Voices' of Radio Nigeria. I was being paid some money. I was very busy, very active. I was even in the Boy's Scout. My mother would tell you I was always leading people who were bigger and older than I was. So even before she died she always said I sang beautifully, and people loved me for my voice. In my secondary school one of my teachers wanted to take me abroad. But I was afraid this might upset my family. So I didn't allow him to see my father.

Q: You were clearly a rebel of all sorts...

Ans: Essentially, you might say that I am a rebel because if there was an injustice, I would fight for the affected group. When I served in present Akwa Ibom sector as a ranger some Igbo soldiers from Aba were going there to kill the people. They would go in lorries to kill the people under the pretence that they were saboteurs. The Ngwa-Aba people would just go and ravage the areas. One of the tasks I was given was to protect the Akwa Ibom neighbours. We were based in Onicha-Ngwa from where we went into the town in Akwa Ibom. When we got to there we discovered that they had all fled into the bush. We searched until we saw a headless corpse. We laid ambush until one person came. He ran and we chased him into the bush. When we got there we saw the whole town inside the bush. I said to them "Ikot Inene is your town, those who said they are fighting the saboteurs were not sent by government. You have a responsibility to come back and defend your town. If any person comes to attack you, kill him." I ordered that they mount check points which they did. And they stopped being victims of the cowards that murdered them.

That was how we ended the terror of the Aba Ngwa-Igbo. After I dealt with the people of Aba they were saying that they didn't know that a fellow Igbo would deal with them that way.

So wherever there is injustice, I will fight against it. That is the way I was brought up. We had no strangers in our house. Everybody was the same. My creativity is highly influenced by this way of life.

Review

Chapter Eight

Sunset, and the Innocent Victims

J.M.Etiowo

INNOCENT Victims is Abubakar Gimba's third novel. It is a story of fraud, abuse of power and political machinery for selfish ends. The action of the novel is centred on Faruk Kolo, and his department of food and animal production, where he is director- general. The setting is the civil service as an institution under a military regime. A panel is set up to probe the activities of the department of food and animal production. Through an examination of the ways and methods of this department and the proceedings of the probe panel, we are made witnesses to the in fighting, power struggle, and corruption that prevail in the civil service.

In *Innocent Victims*, some director-generals like Faruk of the department of food and animal production are perceived to be more powerful than others like Hajj Zaalim of special duties. Through envy and craving for position, Zaalim sets up machinery for intrigues and manipulation of truth to blackmail the department of food and animal production. Zaalim's aim is to have Faruk implicated while the former takes the position of the latter at the end. A board of inquiry is instituted to look into the workings of the Department, and all the 'deviations' that have been committed since its inception. The terms of reference of the panel are: "made vague, formless and watery...so that the main culprits could be let off' (46-47).

From the terms of reference of the panel, one could deduce a vendetta behind the probe rather than a desire to objectively assess the success or otherwise of the department, or as a move to overhaul a failing department. The terms therefore are the official stamp for a witch-hunt and blackmail of the director-general and others at the helm of affairs of the department.

The terms of reference, on their own, become an indictment of the government that has constituted the probe panel and provided its terms. The very short time between when the cabinet meeting decides to set a probe on the activities of Food and Animal Production and when Faruk is given his letter of suspension and when the panel is inaugurated, is equally a statement on the motives and intrigues behind government action.

However, the setting up of the probe panel and her proceedings are the pedestals on which the author stands to pass severe judgment on government, the civil service, civil servants, individuals, security agents and the society at large. The proceedings become an avenue for Gimba's moral sermonising on an evil institution (civil service) or a society in which friends have become villains and betrayers. It is a situation in which positions of power have become abused for sheer personal gains, codes and norms disregarded and corruption and corrupt practices almost accepted and acceptable codes. The testimonies at the panel are revelations about a degenerate civil service that has refused either to serve or to be civil. For instance, the land liaison office is supposed to be in-charge of all land applications and allocations for residential, commercial, industrial, and agricultural lands. One of the rules is that a family residing in a town or city should not be allocated more than three plots of land in that town or city of residence. The processing of the application forms and the subsequent allocation of land should be on a first come, first served basis. But according to the testimony of the deputy lands liaison officer, who is also the secretary of the lands allocation committee, the land allocations regulations are not adhered to in the allocation of lands:

Some individuals and organizations wielding their influence got their applications processed too early to the allocation committee, which promptly approved them. The existing regulations put the maximum number of plot per family at three, in any one town or city where the family is resident.

People owned more than ten such plots in one town. Under false declarations and condoned by the Allocation Committee, people got industrial plots without any thread of connection or even a remote intention to go into setting up any industrial establishment. But worst of all, ... under the guise of agricultural promotion, individuals got large tracts of lands for themselves. So did a handful of companies... a few individuals and organization, because of their connections and political vantage points, have more or less partitioned the choicest lands of the state between themselves. The peasant farmers' interests were not seriously reckoned with. And most of them are no more than tenants on their ancestral lands (121). Those involved in this illegal massive land acquisition "are mostly politicians, a few military officers, and a couple of civil servants" (122).

The implication of the above is that, the original owners of the lands become squatters in their own ancestral lands. Gimba describes the situation as a "whirlwind which our recent political arrangement so licentiously permitted" (Innocent Victims 122). The description of the situation as a whirlwind is a condemnation of the prevailing situation or procedures; the whirlwind is a metaphor for destruction, confusion, and disastrous consequences. Cabinet Office Annex Three is burnt and government property destroyed. Landowners lose their ancestral lands to rich private investors without compensation and Faruk is untimely relieved of his post, among others. And the term 'licentious' depicts the author's derogatory regard for those involved in the land aggrandizement. At the panel it is also revealed that fertilizer procurement and distribution procedures are not done according to government regulations. There is 'wrong timing in the delivery of fertilizers to farmers, retailing by the field staff which are often accounted for as broken bags, selling of the bags above subsidized rates, deliberate curtailment of supplies to village areas that insist on paying government advertised rates as a punitive measure" (125). The testimony of Faruk is the high point of the probe panel's sitting. Faruk is first of all cross-examined by the leading lawyer.

The lawyer's cross-examination seems patterned and predetermined to embarrass Faruk. In his own questioning, the panel chairman, Justice Nuru holds that Faruk being more disposed and inclined to the PWP strategy should have resigned from government when the DAP comes up with a change of policy.

Faruk's cross-examination and responses also depict the author's indictment of the carelessness and misuse of positions of power by the civil servant. For instance, Faruk acquires one hundred hectares of land and two hundred and fifty heads of cattle because the Democratic Alliance Party has told civil servants to turn their backyards into vegetable gardens. But as it is rightly pointed out in the novel one hundred hectares of land is more than a backyard and two hundred and fifty heads of cattle cannot be brought up in a garden (150). Again, Dip's encouragement of private initiative in agriculture is abused. Faruk obtains a certificate of occupancy in his name for six thousand hectares of land belonging to his community. His action is symbolic of office holders' inclination to betray, for selfish reasons, the trust of the people. The result is shameful dispossession of the people whose interest one is sworn to protect simply to promote personal interests.

The ruling government in the novel also comes under Gimba's scrutinizing glare. The military sees herself in governance as on a messianic mission because the civilians/politicians have been 'messing up the country'. The military has intervened to "change things for the better, for the rapid progress of this country" (59). And this they must do "by reason and by force." (59) What we see in Innocent Victims is a military that is brutal, inhuman, arrogant, and insensitive. Squadron Leader Santali Solomon, the military officer sent to oversee the department of food and animal production following the indefinite suspension of Faruk, is representative. Just a few hours after assuming office in the department, he locks out workers who are minutes late to their offices after the lunch break. While the locking out of late civil servants may be commendable as a deterrent, Solomon's verbal and physical insults stand condemnable because it dehumanises and demoralises the individual and the system, and also do not follow laid down civil service regulations which stipulate warnings and queries for offenders. The high point of this brutal drama is the beating into coma the director of agro-industrial projects in the department, Hajj Bala Bakatsoro. Bakatsoro finally dies a few days after from complications arising from the beating. Deserving public officers should be disciplined as a corrective measure and a deterrent against future offenders. But punishment need not enrobe its victims in ridicule, especially for crimes of lateness. When punishment is allowed to degenerate, the system becomes demoralized, and its credibility in the eyes of the public takes a deep plunge. And the society is the loser... Certainly, to line civil servants up early in the morning and rain abuses on them, do frog-jump, or swim on land or such drills, are degrading, humiliating, and ridiculing... such humiliation and degradation are only one step removed from persecution. (74 - 75)

One can say, that Bakatsoro's resistance against Solomon's abuse of power and privilege is a resistance against oppression suppression and humiliation of any kind from whatever source.

As it shall be seen in *Sunset for a Mandarin* the security agents who are meant to be the 'protective shell' of the people turn themselves into the people's enemy, the people's source of agony. Faruk as a Good Samaritan once goes to the Abuja Road Police Station Number Five to report a traffic accident. On reaching the police station, and being disregarded by those on duty, Faruk thinks he should now get the attention of the ASP who has just come in, to report the accident. But the ASP shows little concern; he just calls on a Sergeant to listen to whatever complaints Faruk has. The sergeant on his part takes a long time getting a pen and paper for the purpose of taking down information. At last Faruk is asked his name and address, and requested to make a statement. While people are dying and traffic disrupted, the police always posing as 'friend of the people' is showing blatant insensitivity to the people's plight. Interrogation assumes a different dimension with the police. It is now a synonym for torture and humiliation of mere suspects. A suspect required to report to the police station daily is either made to wait for two to three hours or is left unattended to for the whole day (159). At roadblocks or gates, the police and indeed other security agents constitute themselves into agents of intimidation and insulting behaviours (113-114). From these unbecoming behaviours of the security agents, Gimba concludes that, "these security agents whether at the gates or at road-blocks, whenever they wanted to, anybody not in uniform seemed an enemy to be treated roughly and disdainfully..." (114 -115). The author's view is that this should not be the case, because, a security agent:

> ...just has no case for being irresponsible... There is nothing more nauseating than seeing a public officer, be he in the army, Police or in the civil service, trying to lord it over the very member of the public he is being paid to serve. It is the greatest act of betrayal: more so when a security officer who had sworn to protect the people turns around to threaten and intimidate them for no just cause. Nothing can be more reprehensible. (115 116).

The novel shows that, the "legal system accords truth multiple faces and holds society to ransom because of assumed ignorance" (112). While legal technicalities are employed to win cases, promote chambers, and create wealth for the legal practitioners, social justice should not be perverted in the process:

> ...legal practice must go beyond taking on and winning cases just for the swelling of one's accounts with the banks. A legal practitioner must accord the upholding of social justice a pride of place.
> Therefore, "people must live by some principle and not purse alone". (110)

As in *Victims*, the author seems at home in *Sunset for a Mandarin* where the setting is against the background of a military government. It has been mentioned in *Victims* that the military sees its role in governance as a civilizing, redemptive one. But as we also see in *Sunset* the military is far from performing or achieving those self-perceived roles. The military we find in Sunset for a Mandarin is that which is high- handed, does not appreciate assistance, exalts sycophancy, and is so incensed with power and its use and misuse for self-glory and self-fulfilment. In the novel the sole administrator (SMA) and chief executive officer of Kindendo State represents the military in governance. Hamzah has been in good standing with the SMA who found the former's services reliable. Through intrigues and fabrications Hamzah's treasury department is accused of financial mismanagement. The SMA is particularly irked by the fact that payments he has not approved are made and "the ones I approved they didn't pay…" Hamzah explains:

> …the Treasury Department has to exercise its financial management function to make payments which are urgent and in the interest of the smooth running of the government machineries, and to delay some payments of lesser urgency and priority… (135).

To the SMA, the above explanation or whatever financial management discretion the treasury has to perform is not enough reason why his orders on payment must not be carried out. What the SMA is particular about is that his own financial interests be protected above the interests of the taxpayers or the general public. He orders a financial report.

The report demanded by the SMA is made ready within one week. Rather than scrutinize it and assess the validity or otherwise of its contents for the overall good of the people, it becomes, the platform for victimization. The first fallout of the report is the transfer of Hamzah from the Treasury to the Department of Health. In less than twenty-four hours Hamzah is again transferred to the research and history bureau, the archives unit of the cabinet office. An Assistant Deputy Director normally heads the Research and History Bureau and one is usually sent there on punitive posting. Hamzah as director-general is, therefore, above heading that unit. In addition one may ask what is Hamzah being punished for? Admittedly, the vicious Waleefa plays a major role in the crisis before and after the report, but as a Chief Executive Officer of the State, the SMA should have followed certain procedures to arrive at certain decisions, and not depend on hearsay and on personalized anger.

Neither the cabinet members nor the public know the contents of the report or the relationship or otherwise of the report contents to the issues that gave rise to the report in the first place. In addition, there is no internal audit carried out on the report or an internal administrative inquiry set up to examine the submitted report. Above all, Hamzah has not been presented with facts of allegations neither is he given a chance to defend himself. One therefore is forced to ask: on what does the self-perceived savior -the military here represented by the SMA base his actions? Eight weeks after the report on payments was submitted to the SMA, and without discussing the report with Hamzah, or asking him to defend any aspect of it, the former asks the latter to resign from office. Hamzah is not given any reason why he should put in a resignation letter. The SMA tells Hamzah:

> ...I want your letter of resignation. ...I'm being only fair to you. I could have you dismissed...this is in your best interest...quietly give me your letter, and leave honourably without a bad publicity that would be injurious to you (169).

Like Bakatsoro when pitted against Squadron Leader Solomon in Innocent Victims, Hamzah refuses to bow to intimidation and oppression. He tells the SMA:

> I will not resign…if you want me to leave service now…you are free to give me a letter of termination or even dismissal…to do what you have asked me to do is to tell lies against myself. It'll give the impression that I want to leave…I can't be so unfair to myself. You want me out…do as you please (170).

Hamzah's defiance in this matter is derived from or informed by the unfairness of the SMA and by Hamzah's strong conviction of his innocence:

> He knew he was not fraudulent. He never ruled out the possibility of acts of omission or commission being found out during the period when the Treasury was under his command. He was prepared to accept blame for such faults or errors of human frailties. But he felt that he deserved a fair hearing, even if he were to be given no concessions on grounds of human imperfections (172).

In defying evil he teaches a lesson to the down-trodden: they should refuse to be cowed in the face of exploitation or blatant misapplication of power, by those to whom power has been entrusted. According to Gimba himself:

> …my belief is that people should first prove their suspicion before inflicting punishment on others. And prove them clearly, convincingly even to the suspected…the cause of justice is not harmed by openness to the accused, the guilty: in fact it enhances it. (Sunset…173 174)

The SMA retires Hamzah from the civil service and a letter is issued to him to that effect. The head of government initially could not lay claim to any guilt or misdeed on the part of Hamzah, but at the same time does not just want to "retire him on grounds of services no longer required." Commander Abdud, the SMA, therefore resolves that, "there must be a reason. Convincing reason. A shocking reason... to make Hamzah regret his audacity for the rest of his life" (182). He finds one convincing, shocking reason in the charge of "misappropriation of 14.2 million Songhai Dollars between September and December" (197), against Hamzah. "If he (Hamzah) has the audacity to openly dare me by refusing to resign, I should have the courage to openly tell the people what I think he has done." (184 -185)

The Justice secretary tries to persuade the SMA to drop the charges of corruption against Hamzah, arguing that, "there has been a visible consistence about Hamzah's conduct that we must work very hard to convince the people that man stinks..." and that "in law, what we think is not the important thing. It is the evidence to support what we think that is material" (184-185). What follows, as the SMA's response depicts the readiness of public office holders to falsify situations and circumstances and encourage abuse of official or public trust:

> And are you telling me," began the Commander, visibly losing his temper, "you as a lawyer, cannot prove any wrong doing against Hamzah despite everything I have said? Was I just wasting my saliva...? Look my friend, if Hamzah can't resign, then I will give him a retirement letter with a reason! And that reason will not be a mere for services no longer required. And whatever reason I give be prepared to defend it...! (185)

In his private ruminations without voicing it out Munzir the State Security boss acknowledges that the SMA's actions against Hamzah is akin to murdering him (Hamzah) and destroying him for life:

> You sacked a man, on a serious charge, without giving him a chance to defend himself... A highly tendentious allegation...against an honest man... your friend... and blackening him with a tar brush all over the place... doing him enough damage to destroy him for life. (265)

Admittedly, Hamzah is not an angel, and this much the author and Hamzah himself have acknowledged. But these condemnations, strong as they are, of Commander Abdud's actions are Gimba's own outcry against the violation or sacrifice of the sanctity of humanity, of friendship, at the altar of exercise of power. A recurring factor in these two novels is the uncomplimentary disposition of security and law enforcement agents. These agents are supposed to ensure the security of lives and property, maintain law and order, and if need be, protect the integrity of the nation. But what is seen in Sunset as in *Innocent Victims,* is a security outfit that is not concerned with the security of any life except that of those in positions of power, and law enforcement agents whose only role is the breaking of law and orderliness. Our first contact with the Kindendo state security boss, Hajj Munzir, is in the secret meeting between him, the SMA, Waleefa, Secretary for finance and secretary for treasury. The state security boss has come to brief the SMA on the security situation following Hamzah's retirement. What we find here is that the state security boss does not give the correct security report; what he presents is a false security report. From the text it is obvious the aim is to go after Hamzah, and please the head of government. The police chief advises against the arrest and detention of Hamzah, arguing that there is a need to handle the case with caution. However, Commander Abdud finds a willing hangman in Munzir "Well, if the Police aren't so hospitable as to have him as their guest, I will"(212). Ridiculously, the reason Munzir gives for Hamzah to deserve his 'hospitality' is because Hamzah is "a mystery man of a kind, who has the gullet to gulp down such a whooping amount of money from the public treasury, and in record time...And we being a curious lot, want to know how he performed the feat."(212).

The security boss acknowledges that in "truth...the odds are not so obviously titled in our favour" (that is in the crisis with Hamzah). And so instead of an outright arrest,

> ...my men would invite him to the Intelligence Headquarters for routine questioning.
> Not arrest him. The sessions would last for a whole day, seven days a week. And we can get him to keep on reporting to us with that sort of frequency for the next three months or so, depending on how upright he has been. On the slighted evidence of wrongdoing, we'll detain him (217).

This is a sad statement, an indictment, of an institution entrusted with the security of the people but which has turned itself into the people's nightmare. It also shows the great callousness in requiring a suspect to report to the Security Headquarters continuously every day for three months with no effort made by his accusers to either nail him or exonerate him. While in detention, the State Security boss continues:

> We pamper our guests, massage them so thoroughly that most of them in fact vomit out whatever it was they have taken before their visit to us... But even in such cases, we don't get subjected to public ire... Let us handle him we'll teach him a lesson or two. (213)

If as Munzir confesses, there is little evidence to collaborate their charges against Hamzah, one wonders what lesson the Security outfit has to teach Hamzah and for what purposes. Hamzah goes to New Tymbuktu to see his friend and erstwhile boss, Major Khalid, and give his own side of the crisis. Through intrigue, and falsification of circumstances, Hamzah is invited to headquarters for 'routine' questioning in connection with a "stolen car." The situation at the local security headquarters at New Tymbuktu is worthy of note. According to Munzir, all that happen at Tymbuktu the accusation of Hamzah using a stolen car; the invitation to ISA Headquarters, Ibn Sultan's involvement and subsequent 'drama' at ISA Headquarters; the keeping of Hamzah at District Two Police Station, have been planned by Munzir and his men from Dendiy city. What this implies is that the whole security network is a network of set-ups, a network built on insecurity; it is a network of victimization, a network of brutality, a network of falsehood and deceit, and a network of dehumanisation. The security operatives are arrogant and do not have regard for time factor or discomfort of their guests. They see themselves as unchallengeable little gods, who "don't seem bothered by keeping lesser mortals whose interest they, the gods, are employed and paid to protect, waiting on end." (247).

Hamzah's encounter with the state security and his detention is the peak of injustice in this melodrama. An acclaimed righteous or innocent man is unjustly treated, for reasons other than that for which the security outfit has been established. According to Munzir:

> The objective is to get him to talk about his retirement from the service...entrap him to make some confessional statements... which we could use against him, in need... It's very

necessary...The guy is surely not an angel, but his file with us certainly gives us no room to swoop on him, as we would on any blackguard with just one-tenth the stinking stain this guy has been accused of. (264)

Hamzah's case is a symbolic representation of the fate of the innocent citizenry in the hands of the state security.

The police in Sunset is another law enforcement agency whose conduct does not befit its status, and which the author's moral eye does not overlook. A young man is unlawfully arrested for a crime, he did not commit, taken to the police station and severely beaten up. At 4a.m. when the young man begins to vomit blood, the murderous mind of the policemen is vividly described:

> The two corporals said he could swim in his blood if he cared to vomit enough. Or drink it. It was not till 6.30a.m. when an ASP came that the young man was rushed to the hospital. And by mid-day, the young man had died. The cause of death according to the result of the autopsy performed, was internal bleeding from the battering. (78)

The death of the young man from police brutality shows how "a body entrusted with the protection of its citizenry is turning into a dreaded, awesome assailant of the same citizenry" (81). As if the death of the young man is not enough, the Police Public Relations Unit comes out with a defensive and false version of the incident, calculated to deceive. However, the young policemen are to be charged to court and persecuted for culpable homicide. The promotion of the ASP who condemns the actions of his colleagues and the police commissioner who stands for the truth are Gimba's testimony to the fact that those who uphold the sanctity of

178

power should be rewarded for having the courage to perform their duties in the face of tremendous odds.

Notes and Bibliography

Chapter One
Literature and Leadership Issues

Works Cited

Achebe, Chinua. *Anthills of the Savannah*. Ibadan: Heinemann Books, 1988.

– – –. *Morning Yet on Creation Day*. London: Heinemann Books, 1975.

– – –. *No Longer at Ease*. Ibadan: Heinemann Books, 1960.

– – –. *The Trouble with Nigeria*. Enugu: Fourth Dimension, 1984.

Adewale, Toyin. Naked Testimonies. Lagos: Mace Books, 1995.

Armah, Ayi Kwei. *The Beautyful Ones are not Yet Born*. London: Heinemann, 1985.

Bassey, Nnimo. *We Thought it was Oil but it was Blood*. Ibadan: Kraftgriots, 2002.

Ce, Chin. *An African Eclipse*. Enugu: Handel Books, 2000.

– – –.*Children of Koloko*. Enugu: Handel Books, 2001.

CODESRIA (The Council for Development of Social Science Research in Africa) MWG. Introduction, 2004.

Enekwe, Ossie. *Broken Pots*. Nsukka: Afa Press, 2004.

Osundare, *Niyi. Songs of the Market Place*. Ibadan: New Horn, 1983.

Onwubiko, K.B.C. *History of West Africa*. Onitsha: Africana-Fep Publishers, 1973

Peacock, H. L. *A History of Modern Europe*. London: Heinemann, 1982.

Shakespeare, William. *Macbeth*. London: Longman, 1979.

Soyinka, Wole. *The Beatification of an Area Boy*. Ibadan: Spectrum, 2001.

Trask, David. *American Reader*. Ed. Leo Lemay. Washington: USIA, 1988.

Chapter Two
Africa in the Narratives of Laurence

Note

1.Von Trieschke was a savvy and renowned German scholar. The statement is taken from a series of public lectures he gave to graduate students in universities at Munich and Bonn in late 19th century but was published only in 1914.

Works Cited

Achebe, Chinua. "An Image of Africa: Racism in Conrad's Heart of Darkness." *Hopes and Impediments*. New York: Double Day, 1989.

Bourdieu, Pierre. *The Field of Cultural Production*. Ed. Randal Johnson.New York: Columbia University Press, 1993.

Collu, Gabrielle. "Writing About Other: The African Stories." *The Writings of Margaret Laurence: Challenging Territories*. Ed. Riegel Christian. Edmonton: University of Alberta Press, 1997.

Day, Richard. *Multiculturalism and the History of Canadian Diversity*. Toronto: Toronto University Press, 2000.

Echeruo, Michael. *Joyce Cary and the Novel of Africa*. London: Longmans, 1973.

Fournie, Suzanne and Ernie Crey. *Stolen From Our Embrace: The Abduction of First Nations Children and the Restoration Of Aboriginal Communities*. Vancouver, Toronto: Douglass and McIntyre Ltd., 1997.

Friskney, B. Janet. "The Many Aspects of a General Editorship: Malcolm Ross and the NCL." *Canadian Poetry. 52* (2003).

Groening, Laura. "Malcolm Ross and the New Canadian Library: Making Real or Making a Difference?" *Studies in Canadian Literature 25:1* (2000). 95-110.

Githae-Mugo, Micere. *Visions of Africa: The Fiction of Chinua Achebe, Margaret Laurence, Elspeth Huxley and Ngugi Wa Thiongo*. Nairobi: Kenya Literature Bureau, 1978.

Hjartarson, Paul and Tracy Kulba. "'Born Across the World': Else Plotz (Baroness Elsa von Freytag-Loringhoven), Felix Paul Greve (Fredrick Philip Grove), and the Politics of Cultural Mediation." *The Politics of Cultural Mediation*. Eds. Paul Hjartarson and Tracy Kulba. Edmonton, University of Alberta, Press, 2003.

Henderson, M.O. *The German Colonial Empire:1884-1919*. London: Frank Cass Ltd., 1993.

Killam, D.G. "Introduction." *This Side Jordan*. Toronto: McClelland and Stewart Ltd., 1960.

Laurence, Margaret. "Ten Years' Sentences." *A Place To Stand On: Essays By and About Margaret Laurence*. Ed. George Woodcock. Edmonton: Newest Press, 1983.

---. *Long Drums and Cannons: Nigerian Dramatists and Novelists1952-1966*. Ed. Nora Stovel. Edmonton: University of Alberta Press, 2001.

---. *A Tree For Poverty*. Ontario: McMaster University Library Press, 1993.

181

---. *The Prophet's Camel Bell.* Toronto: McClelland and Stewart, 1963.

---. *This Side Jordan.* Toronto: McClelland and Stewart, 1960.

---. *The Tomorrow-Tamer and Other Stories.* Toronto: McClelland and Stewart, 1970.

---. *Heart of a Stranger.* Ed. Nora Stovel. Edmonton: University of Alberta, Press, 2003.

Lindfors, Bernth, Ian Munro, Richard Priebe, and Reinhard Sander, eds. Palaver: *Interviews With Five African Writers in Texas.* Austin: The University of Texas Press, 1972.

Little, Kenneth. *The Sociology of Urban Women's Image in African Literature. London and Basingstoke*: The Macmillan Press LTD, 1980.

Lecker, Robert. Making It Real: *The Canonization of English-Canadian Literature.* Ontario: House of Anansi Press Ltd., 1995.

----. "The Canadian Block Grant Program and the Construction of the Canadian Literature". *English Studies in Canada.* 25:3-3(1994). 399-469.

Na'Allah, Abdul-Rasheed. "Nigerian Literature: Then and Now." *Long Drums and Cannons.* Ed. Nora Stovel. Edmonton: University of Alberta Press, 2001.

Pell, Barbara. "The African and Canadian Heroines: From Bondage to Grace." *Challenging Territories.* Ed. Christian Riegel. 1997.

Riegel, Christian. "Introduction: Recognizing the Multiplicity of the Oeuvre". *The Writings of Margaret Laurence: Challenging Territories.* Ed. Christian Riegel. Edmonton: University Of Alberta Press, 1997.

----. "Foreword". *Long Drums and Cannons.* Ed. Nora Stovel Edmonton: University of Alberta Press, 2001.

Rimmer, Mary. "(Mis) Speaking: Laurence Writes Africa." *The Writings of Margaret Laurence: Challenging Territories.* Ed. Christian Riegel.Alberta: University of Alberta, Press, 1993.

Sparrow, Fiona. *Into Africa With Margaret Laurence.* Toronto: ECW Press, 1992.

Sullivan, Rosemary. "An Interview With Margaret Laurence." Ed. George Woodcock. Newest Press, 1983.

Stovel, Nora. "Heart of A Traveler: Margaret Laurence Life's Journey." *Heart of a Stranger.* Alberta: University of Alberta Press, 2003.

Tapping, Craig. " Margaret Laurence and Africa." *Crossing the River: Essays in Honour of Margaret Laurence.* Ed. Kristjana Gunnars. Manitoba: Turnstone Press,1988.

Thomas, Clara. "After words." *The Prophet's Camel Bell*. Margaret Laurence. Ontario: New Canadian Library, 1988.

---- "Morning Yet On Creation Day: A Study of This Side Jordan". *A Place to Stand On*. George Woodcock Ed. Edmonton: NeWest Press, 1983.

Watts, Cedric. "Introduction." *Heart of Darkness and other Tales*. Oxford: Oxford University Press, 1991.

Walsh, William. "Preface." *A Manifold Voice: Studies in Common Wealth Literature*. New York: Barns and Noble Inc., 1970.

Xiques, Donez. "Introduction.' *A Tree For Poverty: Somali Poetry and Prose*. Margaret Laurence (collected). Ontario: Mcmaster University Library Press, 1993.

Chapter Three
The Literary Economy of *Congo Diary*

Notes

1. Conrad's The Congo Diary, as it has come to be known, consists of two notebooks. The second notebook, entitled "Up-river Book", begins on 3rd August 1890, and records his journey up the Congo on board the steamer, Roi des Belges. It contains mostly maps and navigational information; and therefore has little narrative or literary interest. The text of the first notebook, the diary proper (on which this paper is based) was first published in an edited and annotated form by Richard Curle in the magazine, *The Blue Peter* in 1925, and then again in his edition of Conrad's pieces entitled *Last Essays* in 1926. All references to the diary are to Richard Curle's edition of "The Congo Diary" collected in *Conrad's Tales of Hearsay and Last Essays*. London: Dent, 1926.

2. Shortland has usefully shown how, indeed, physiognomy "deals with man's character and stable features"; and how, in other words, the physiognomist defines her "perceptual field as those stable parts of the body observable from the exterior" (Shortland 28).

3. The very notion or concept of the gaze implies an "economy", not only in the sense of a structure of hierarchy of political power but also of the investigation of the "wealth" of a specimen, and its uses for the good of human beings. According to Spary, 18th century European natural historians discussed nature and bodies in economic terms, and in terms of the hierarchy or distribution of political power and other social energies (Spary 178).

4. The term "visualism" was coined by Johannes Fabian to describe a form of Western ethnographic knowledge which is based on visual observation and on the (text-based) production of spatial images, maps, diagrams, trees and tables, so that non-Western cultures are viewed as synchronic (fixed, static)

objects of visual perception. On this, see Fabian, Time and the Other; Fabian, "Presence and Representation".

5. We are indebted to Karl Marx for this phrase. In the *Economic and Philosophical Manuscripts* of 1844, Marx also speaks of nature as being man's body without organ: "Man lives from nature, i.e. it his body, and must remain in a continuous process with it if he is not to die... man is a part of nature" (328). The point is that for Conrad of the diary, it is the native body, not nature (as it is for Marx), which is the paradoxical Subject, a dumb generality, without voice-consciousness. (On this, see Marx 326-30; Scarry 243-60; Spivak 76-7; Eagleton 196-230).

6. In the Western imperial history and neo-Hegelian philosophy, stone monuments are a powerful marker of civilization and human freedom, as can be seen in the controversy over whether black, rather than white, people built the great Zimbabwe, a stone ruins in modern Zimbabwe. Following the example of Hegel in Lectures on the Philosophy of World History, Lord Lugard, the early colonial administrator of Nigeria, viewed many African communities as uncivilized since they had not, unlike the great Egyptians, for example, left behind any stone monuments or buried cities. (See, on this, Hegel 174; Lugard 1-5).

7. This is the view one finds in critics of Achebe's critique of Conrad's representation of black people in *Heart of Darkness*. Here Achebe calls Conrad a "bloody racist." Achebe argues that Conrad in *Heart of Darkness* constructs Africa as "a metaphysical battlefield, devoid of all recognizable humanity, into which the European enters at his peril... It was and is the dominant image of Africa in the Western imagination" (Achebe 788-792). (For a review of the debate, for and against Achebe's view, see Harrison, Postcolonial Criticism 22-61).

8. The term différance (note the "a") was coined in 1968 by the French philosopher and literary critic, Jacques Derrida (1930--2004). It denotes a sense of deferral, of difference differed. Its other meaning is deferment (to defer and to differ). It is used by Derrida to convey the notion that the play of signification is, and can only be, constantly deferred, never fully achieved. It refers to the endless spillage, slipping, and sliding of language and meaning. In Derrida's special usage, Differánce is neither a word nor a concept, but a radically unstable term which disrupts systematization, for example, a conceptual centre or a logical origin. See, on this, Derrida, Margins 3 and Positions 77.

Works Cited

Achebe, Chinua. "An Image of Africa: Racism in Conrad's Heart of Darkness." *Massachusetts Review* 18.4 (1977): 782-94.

Barthes, Roland. "From Work to Text." *Debating Texts*. Ed. Rick Rylance. Milton Keynes: Open University, 1987. 117-22.

Bhabha, Homi. *The Location of Culture*. London: Routledge, 1994.

Bourdieu, Pierre. *Distinction: A Social Critique of the Judgment of Taste*. Trans. R. Nice. Cambridge, Mass.: Harvard U P, 1984.

Brantlinger, Patrick. "The Rule of Darkness." *Literary Theory: An Anthology* Eds. J. Rivkin and M. Ryan.. New York: Basil Blackwell, 1998. 856-67.

Carr, Helen. "Modernism and Travel." *The Cambridge Companion to Travel Writing*. Eds. Peter Hulme and Tim Youngs. Cambridge: Cambridge U P, 2002. 70-86.

Derrida, Jacques. *Of Grammatology*. Baltimore MD: Johns Hopkins University Press, 1976.

– – – . *Writing and Difference*. Chicago: The U of Chicago P, 1978.

– – – . *Positions*. Trans. Alan Bass, Chicago: Chicago U P, 1981.

– – – . *Margins of Philosophy*. Trans. Alan Bass, Chicago: Chicago U P, 1982.

Duncan, James. "Dis-Orientation: On the Shock of the Familiar in a Faraway Place." *Writers of Passage: Reading Travel Writing*. Eds. J. Duncan and D. Gregory. London: Routledge, 1999. 151-63

Eagleton, Terry. *The Ideology of the Aesthetic*. Oxford: Blackwell, 1990.

Fabian, Johannes. *Time and the Other: How Anthropology Makes its Object*. New York: Columbia U P, 1983.

– – – . "Presence and Representation: the Other in Anthropological Writing." *Critical Inquiry 16* (1990): 753-72.

Foucault, Michel. *The Order of Things: An Archaeology of the Human Sciences*. New York: Vintage, 1970.

Gilman, Sander. *Difference and Pathology*. Ithaca, NY: Cornell UP.

Hall, Stuart. "The Spectacle of the Other." *Representation: Culture Representations and Signifying Practices*. Ed. Stuart Hall. London: Sage Publications, 1997. 223-279.

Hampson, Robert. *Joseph Conrad: Betrayal and Identity*. Basingstoke: Macmillan, 1992.

Hawkins, Hunt. "Conrad and Congolese Exploitation." *Conradiana 13* (1981): 94-99.

Hegel, Wilhelm Friedrich. *Lectures on the Philosophy of World History*, Cambridge: Cambridge U P, 1975.

Hochschild, Adam. *King Leopold's Ghost*. New York: Houghton Mifflin, 1998.

Jean-Aubry, Gerald. *Conrad in the Congo*. London: Bookman's Journal, 1926.

Knowles, Owen and Gene M. Moore. Oxford Reader's Companion to Conrad. Oxford: Oxford U P.

Lidchi, H. "Politics of Exhibiting Other Cultures." *Representation: Cultural Representations and Signifying Practices.* Ed. Stuart Hall. London: Sage Publications, 1997. 151-222.

Low, Chin-Lian. "His Stories? Narratives and Images of Imperialism." *New Formations 12* (1990): 97-123.

Lugard, J. Dealtry. *The Dual Mandate in British Tropical Africa.* London: Frank Cass, 1965.

Marx. Karl. *Early Writings.* Ed. Lucio Coletti. Penguin: Harmondsworth, 1975.

Mercer, Kobena. "Imaging the Black Man's Sex." *Male Order: Unwrapping Masculinity.* Ed. R. Chapman and J. Rutherford. London: Lawrence and Wishart, 1988.

Najder, Zdzislaw. Ed. *Joseph Conrad Congo Diary and Other Uncollected Pieces.* Garden City, NY: Doubleday and Company, 1978.

Pfeiffer, Ludwig. "The Black Hole of Culture: Japan, Radical Otherness, and the Disappearance of Difference." *The Translatability of Cultures: Figurations of the Space Between.* Eds. S. Budick and W. Iser. Stanford: Stanford U P, 1996. 186-203.

Pratt, Mary Louis. Imperial Eyes: *Travel Writing and Transculturation.* London: Routledge, 1997.

Scarry, Elaine. *The Body in Pain: The Making and Unmaking of the World.* Oxford: Oxford U P, 1985.

Sherry, Norman. *Conrad's Western World.* Cambridge: Cambridge U P, 1971.

Shortland, Michael. "Skin Deep: Barthes, Lavater, and the Legible Body." *Ideological Representation and Power in Social Relations.* Ed. Mike Gane. London: Routledge, 1989. 17-54.

Spary, Emma. "Political, Natural and Bodily Economies." *Cultures of Natural History.* Eds. N. Jardine, J.A. Secord, and E.C. Spary. Cambridge: Cambridge UP, 1996. 178-96.

Spivak, Gayatri Chakravorty. *Critique of Post-Colonial Reason: Toward a History of the Vanishing Present.* Cambridge, Mass. Harvard U P, 1999.

Spurr, David. *The Rhetoric of Empire: Colonial Discourse in Journalism, Travel Writing and Imperial Administration.* Durham: Duke U P, 1996.

Youngs, Tim. "Africa/The Congo: The Politics of Darkness." *The Cambridge Companion to Travel Writing.* Eds. Peter Hulme and Tim Youngs. Cambridge: Cambridge U P, 2002. 156-1.

Chapter Four
Apport de l'œuvre de Jacques Roumain

Reference

Iheanacho, Egonu. « René Maran : Point de depart de la Nouvelle Literature Africaine en langue Française.Revue de la litterature et d'esthethique negro-africain, Abdijan : Nouvelles Editions. Afrcaines,1982,p.7.

Lezou, Gerard Dago. La Création Romanesque devant les transformations actuelles en Cote d'Ivoire.Abdijan : Nouvelles Editions Africaines, 1972,p.68.

Zeraffa, Michel. Roman et Société. Paris : Presses Universitaires de France, 1971,p.20.

Millspaugh, Arthur. Haiti under American control 1915-1930. Boston Massachusetts : World Peace Foundation, 1931, p.14. Œuvres de Jacques Roumain : La Montagne Ensorcelée. Sans Lieu : Club d'Afrique Loisirs, 1980.

La Proie et L'Ombre paru dans La Montagne Ensorcelée, Sans Lieu : Club d'Afrique Loisirs, 1980

Poèmes paru dans La Montagne Ensorcelée. Sans Lieu : Club d'Afrique Loisirs, 1980.

Gouverneurs de la Rosée. Paris :Editeurs Français Réunis, 1964

Jacques Roumain. La Montagne Ensorcelée.

Anozie cite par Nantet Jacques. Panorama de la Littérature noire d'expression francaise. Paris : Librairie Fayard, 1972, p.240. Jacques Roumain. La Proie et L'Ombre.

Hoffmann, Léon François. Le Nègre Romantique. Paris : Payot, 1973, p.102.

Jacques, Roumain. Gouverneurs de la Rosée.

Conturie, Christiane. Comprendre Gouverneurs de la Rosée de Jacques Roumain.Versailles : Les Classiques Africains, 1992.

Jacques, Roumain. Gouverneurs de la Rosée.

Sartre, Jean Paul. Qu'est-ce que la Littérature? Paris: Gallimard.

J.M.Dash. « The Peasant Novel in Haïti, » African Littérature Today, No.9, 1978.

Sartre, Jean Paul. Qu'est-ce que La Littérature?.

L.N. Nwokora. « Méfiance et Entente Inter-Ethnique en Afrique; Le Défi de la littérature » Paper presented at 3rd NUFTA Conference, Abia State University 2000.

Malraux, André. La Condition Humaine. Paris :Gallimard, 1946, p.136.

Nnolim, Charles. Approaches to the African Novel. PortHarcourt : Saros, 1992.

Chapter Five
The Feminist Impulse

Works Cited

Dlamini, Lucy Z. *The Amaryllis*. Manzini Swaziland: Macmillan Boleswa Publishers (Pty) Ltd., 2001.

Ousmane, Sembene. *Gods Bits of Wood*. London: Heinemann Education Books Ltd., 1970.

Bestman, Martin. "Sembene Ousmane : Social Commitment and the Search for an African Identity." *A Celebration of Black and African Writing*, eds. King and Ogungbesan. Zaria Nigeria: Ahmadu Bello University Press, 1975.

Gates, Henry Louis, Jr., ed. *Reading Black, Reading Feminist : A Critical Anthology*. New York : Meridian Books, 1990.

Hernton, Calvin C. *The Sexual Mountain and Black Women Writers Adventures in Sex, Literature and Real Life*. New York: Anchor Press, 1987.

Ikiriko, Ibiwari. "Ousmane's Achievement in God's Bits of Wood" (an M.A. Thesis presented to the Department of English and Literary Studies, University of Calabar, Calabar-Nigeria, April 1983).

Killam, G.D. , ed. "Interview with Ousmane." *African Writers on African Writing*. London: Heinemann Educational Books, 1973. Mnthali, Felix. *Yoranivyoto* . Glasgow: Dudu Nsomba, 1998.

Mogu, Francis Ibe. *Black Male Writing and Black Female Responses in the United States*. Calabar: Centaur Press, 2002.

– – – A Review of Dlamini's The Amaryllis (Unpublished Mss) Department of English Language and Literature, University of Swaziland, Kwaluseni Swaziland, November, 2003.

– – – Literature and Revolution: A Study of Sembene Ousmane's God's Bits of Wood." (unpublished Mss), April, 1990.

188

Nnaemeka, Obioma, ed. *Sisterhood, Feminisms and Power: From Africa to the Diaspora.* Trenton, New Jersey: Africa World Press, 1998.

Ogundipe-Leslie, Omolara. "The Female Writer and Her Commitment," in Women. *African Literature Today*, *vol. 15*, eds. Eldred Durosimi Jones, Eustace Palmer and Majorie Jones. Trenton, N.J: Africa World Press, 1987.

Ruthven, K.K. *Feminist Literary Studies: An Introduction.* Cambridge: Cambridge University Press, 1984.

Washington, Mary Helen. "The Darkened Eye Restored: Notes Towards a Literary History of Black Women." *Reading Black, Reading Feminist: A Critical Anthology*, ed. Henry Louis Gates, Jr. New York: Meridian, 1990.

Chapter Six
Ngugi's Marxist Aesthetics

Works Cited

Ake, Claude, 'Devaluing Democracy.' Journal of Democracy. Vol. 3, No. 3, July, 1992

Balibar, Etienne and Pierre Macherey. 'On Literature as an Ideological Form.' In Mulhern (ed) Contemporary Marxist Literary Criticism. London and New York: Longman, 1992

Baxter, Joan,. 'Burying Capitalism.' BBC Focus on Africa. April June, 2002

Daniels, Robert V.'Marxism.' The Encyclopedia Americana (International edition). Vol.18. Danbury, Connecticut: Grolier Incorporated, 1997

Ikiddeh, Ime. 'Forward.' In Ngugi wa Thiong'o. Homecoming: Essays on Africa and Caribbean Literature, Culture and Politics. London: Heinemann, 1972

Kim, Kyung-won, 'Marx, Schumpeter, and The East Asian Experience.' Journal of Democracy. Vol. 3, No. 3, July, 1992

Langdon, Steve, 'Multinational Corporations, Taste Transfer and Under-development: A case study from Kenya' RAPE, No. 2.1975

Marx, Karl. Selected Writings in Sociology and Social Philosophy. T.B. Bottomore and Maximilien Rubel (eds). England: Penguin Books, 1956

Marx, Karl and Frederick Engels. Selected Works. Moscow: Progress Publishers, 1968

Ngugi wa Thiong'o. Homecoming: Essays on Africa and Caribbean Literature, Culture and Politics. London: Heinemann, 1972

– – – . Petals of Blood. Nigeria: Heinemann Educational Books, 1977

– – – Writers in Politics. London: Heinemann.

– – – .Decolonising the Mind: The Politics of Language in African Literature. London: James Currey, 1981.

– – – Moving the Centre: The Struggle for Cultural Freedoms. London: James Currey; Nairobi: EAEP; Portsmouth, N.H: Heinemann, 1993

Nkrumah, Kwame. Neo-Colonialism: The Last Stage of imperialism. London: Panaf, 1965

Onoge, Omafume F.. 'The Crisis of Consciousness in Modern African Literature.' In George M. Gulgelberger (ed.) Marxism and African Literature. London: James currey, 1985

Ripstein, Arthur. 'Political Philosophy.' In John V. Canfield (ed.) Routledge History of Philosophy: Philosophy of Meaning Knowledge and Value in the Twentieth Century. Vol. x, London and New York: Routledge, 1997

Ryan, Alan. 'Political Philosophy.' In A.C. Grayling (ed.) Philosophy 2: Further Through the Subject. Oxford: University Press, 1998

Simpson, Chris, 'Sowing the Seeds.' BBC Focus on Africa. July September 2002

So, Alvin Y. Social Change and Development: Modernization, Dependency and World-System Theories. Newbury Park: Sage Publications, 1990

Thomson, Alex. An Introduction to African Politic: London and New York: Routledge. 2000

Townshend, Jules. The Politics of Marxism: The Critical Debates. London: Leicester University Press. 1996

Wallis, William, 'Girdlock.' BBC Focus on Africa. April June. 2002

Weffort, Francisco C. 'The Future of socialism.' Journal of Democracy. Vol.3, No. 3. July 1992

Chapter Seven
Functionalism and African Literature

Works Cited

Adeniji Olayiwola "The Marks of Carnage: A Review of The Last Battle and other Stories." *The Guardian.* 29 July 1996.

Adimeba, Don. "Enekwe's Broken Pots is here at last: A Review. *The Guardian.* 3 Nov. 1986.

Ajao, Toyin "Come Thunder: Another Perspective of the civil War." *The Guardian.* 14 September 1985.

Ajayi, Sesan. "Of Faith not Broken" *The Guardian.* 3 December 1989.

Ajibade Kunle "The Compassionate Story of Onuora Enekwe the 48 year old Nigerian Poet. *African Concord.* 6 May 1991.

Ajibade, Kunle "I would have ended up a Musician." An Interview with O O Enekwe. *Weekend Concord.* 18 May, 1991.

Ayejina, Funso "The Poetry of Enekwe and Udechukwu: Two of a Kind" The Guardian, 19 April 1986.

Chiazo Chi and Chukwuemeka Agbayi "The Colour of Writing" *The Guardia.,* 6 July 1998.

Ezeh, P.J "A Guitar boy's Metamorphosis." *The Post Express.* 26 Sept 1998.

Edith Ihekweazu, "Triumph of a Hero: Ngugi's play at UNN Convocation". *Times Union* 16 February 1978.

Ikwuemesi, Krydz C. "Heroes and Songs - An Introduction to a Commemorative Exhibition on Ossie Enekwe." *Sunday Vanguard.* 14 June 1998.

Ohaeto, Ezenwa "Art Personality: Ossie Enekwe" *Daily Times.* 27 April 1991.

Osundare, Niyi "The Fighting Spirit" (Review of Presentation of Kimathi at Unibadan). *West Africa.* 14 May 1984.

Books by Ossie Onuorah Enekwe

Broken Pots (1977)
Come Thunder (1984)
Igbo Masks: The Oneness of Ritual and Theatre (1987)
The Last Battle and Other Stories (1996)
Trail in the Mines (2000)
Marching to Kilimanjaro (2004)

Chapter Eight
Sunset, and the *Innocent Victims*

Works Cited

Ayandele, Emmanuel, *The Educated Elite in the Nigerian Society.* Ibadan: University Press, 1974.

Etiowo, Joy, "The Moral Vision in Selected Novels of Abubakar Gimba." Unpublished M.A.Thesis of the Department of English and Literary Studies, University of Calabar. 1994.

Fajenyo, E. and O. Esunde, *The Writings of Abubakar Gimba: A Critical Appraisal.* Enugu: Delta, 1994.

Gimba, Abubakar. *Innocent Victims.* Enugu: Delta, 1988.

– – – *Sunset for a Mandarin.* Lagos: West African Books, 1991.

Okpiliya, J. and A. Eyang. "The Civil Service in Fiction: The Ways of Bureaucracy in Gimba's Sunset for a Mandarin" *Ndunode 4.1* 2003

Post Colonial Identities

POSTCOLONIAL Identities
revisits issues regarding the newer
literatures within this expansive African
heritage of diverse regional and national
groupings. We have aimed at
substantiating the cultural uniformity of
Africa in terms of literary and cultural
movements and lending some inter-
disciplinary insights to Africa's prolific
body of literature as a whole through the
complex course of its twentieth
century history. Recognizing the
complexity of Black cultures can help to
understand the cultural, economic, and
political relationships between Africa and
her Diaspora. An imaginative critical
evaluation comes in the 'eclectic
approach' to new oeuvres which, with
the inclusion of hitherto exclusive forms
(poetry and fiction) as one whole
movement of 'dialogue,' 'transition' and
'memory,' adds an important dimension
to the understanding of the remarkable
voices from Africa. The counterpoint of
this work comes up in the entries which
differ in their opinions on the vision and
craft of two post-colonial writers of
Indian and African ethnicities. Finally,
our review of the problems of African
modernity in relation to the concept
of 'Black Atlantic' definitely makes an
impressive finale for these studies.

African
Library of
Critical Writing

SMITH AND CE [ED]

Post
Colonial
Identities

Liberian professor of African
languages and literature,
founder of the Society of
African Folklore, and
Literary Society
International, LSi, Charles
Smith, is editor of the
Critical Writing Series on
African Literature with
Nigerian Chin Ce, books,
news, reviews editor and
research and creative writer.
As one of the younger stream
of poets from Africa, Ce is
also the author of several
works of fiction and essays
on African and Caribbean
literature.

African Books Network

AFRICAN Books Network with its cosmopolitan outlook is poised to meet the book needs of African generations in times to come. Since the year 2000 when we joined the highway of online solutions in publishing and distribution, our African alliance to global information development excels in spite of challenges in the region. Our select projects have given boost to the renaissance of a whole generation of dynamic literature. In our wake is the harvest of titles that have become important referrals in contemporary literary studies. With print issues followed by eContent and eBook versions, our network has demonstrated its commitment to the vision of a continent bound to a common heritage. This universal publishing outlook is further evidenced by our participation in African Literature Research projects. For everyone on deck, a hands-on interactive is the deal which continues to translate to more flexibility in line with global trends ensuring that African writers are part of the information gobalisation of the present.

As one of Africa's mainstream book publishing and distribution networks, many authors may look to us for to privileged assistance regarding affiliate international and local publishing and distribution service

"Our select projects at African Books Network have given boost to the renaissance of a whole generation of dynamic literature."